beautiful forever
Aesthetic Business Consulting

D0596548

Beautifully Profitable
Forever Profitable

The CEO of *beautiful forever* Demonstrates How Effective *Management & Marketing* Can Transform Any Aesthetics Practice or Med-Spa into a *Profitable & Rewarding* Venture

By Cheryl Whitman, CEO
beautiful forever

© 2015

Beautifully Profitable - Forever Profitable. © Copyright 2015 by Cheryl Whitman. All rights reserved. Printed in the United States of America. No part of this book may be used or reproduced in any manner whatsoever without written permission except in the case of brief quotations embodied in critical articles and reviews. For information contact Cheryl Whitman, cheryl@beautifulforever.com, www.beautifulforever.com, www.beautifullyprofitable.com.

ISBN: 978-0-615-95111-9 (Soft Cover) Third Edition

"Shortly after instituting the Day Spa Association in the early 90s Cheryl came to introduce herself with some revolutionary ideas which she quickly materialized and perfected for the past 20+ years.

She emerged to be the expert in skincare ingredients formulations and how to apply this knowledge to empower the medical community to embrace skincare in their medical practice. What she found was a lack of knowledge how to apply these new modalities effectively into the existing as well as newly established facilities to make them efficient and profitable. With her quick mind and incredible foresight, she quickly changed directions and developed methods and formulas for creating profitable entities throughout the US and beyond.

When it became time to form the International Medical Spa Association, she was one of the first that I contacted to become a Founding Member and a Member of the Board of Directors.

Beautiful Forever now has a Beautifully Profitable addition to be used as a reference book that reflects everything that Ms. Whitman recommends to achieve what every spa owner and medical esthetic practice should strive for to become and stay profitable without compromising patients/guests benefits and safety.

I recommend this reference book to be "The Handbook" for the Medical Esthetic Community."

Hannelore Leavy, Principle - HR Leavy LLC, Spa & Wellness Business Consultancy – Communication & Marketing, Founder, Day Spa Association 1991, Executive Director till 2009, Founder, International Medical Spa Association 2002, Executive Director till 2009, Co-Author, The Spa Encyclopedia 2002, Publisher, The Day Spa / Medical Spa Directory 1995-2008, Publisher, The Day Spa /Medical Spa Business Bible 2004

"Cheryl Whitman and her team of consultants were of great help to me in setting up and coordinating my consulting business. My company would never be where it is today without Cheryl's extraordinary business savvy. Thank you Beautiful Forever!"

Dr. Janet Brill, Ph.D. Nutrition & Fitness Expert, Writer, Speaker, Spokesperson, Consultant, Educator

"Having worked closely with Cheryl Whitman over the past ten years to help our multi-specialty group practice grow and meet the demands of an ever evolving marketplace has been a great asset to us. In her book, Beautifully Profitable, she details many of the ways to align services, operations and marketing to ensure profitability. We have utilized her methodologies with great success and with this new book, many other doctors and practice will benefit from her vast experience."

Steve Watson, Founder & CEO – Miami Institute for Age Management and Intervention

"As healthcare continues to evolve, physicians and hospitals need to look for new ways to partner. Wellness is a great area for this partnership. This allows all parties to grow and flourish in areas more and more patients are looking for without having government oversight. As more doctors become aware that their practices are also retail businesses, they will find great help from Cheryl Whitman's new book, Beautifully Profitable. In this, she guides doctors – and yes, hospital executives – on the business and marketing side of healthcare. Her focus is on aesthetics care, but her message applies much more widely."

Bob Haley, FACHE, Executive Director, Rainy Lake Medical Center, Minnesota

"I came to know Cheryl Whitman several years ago through her informative marketing presentations at some of my professional medical meetings. Since then our professional relationship has grown through multiple conversations which eventually led to enlisting her services to do some preliminary MediSpa development work. I have found Cheryl Whitman and the Beautiful Forever staff to be very knowledgeable, sincere and helpful and to have extensive expertise and experience in the practical details of developing a MediSpa."

Christopher R. Hubbell, M.D., FAAD , Lafayette Lousianna , Founder and Medical Director
*Acadiana Dermatology, APMC , *a Jeuné Medical Spa

"In the Aesthetics industry, Cheryl Whitman's name unquestionably rises to the top. Looking back and having known Cheryl for nearly ten years, I wish I had access to a resource like "Beautifully Profitable, Forever Profitable" when I set out to launch my Hair Restoration practice back in 1997.

For physicians and others navigating the highly competitive aesthetic marketplace or looking for that head-start without having to rely on "the school of hard knocks" like we did, I recommend you get to know Cheryl! I strongly recommend her new book, Beautifully Profitable."

Alan J. Bauman, M.D., Diplomate, American Board of Hair Restoration Surgery - Medical Director, Bauman Medical Group - Hair Restoration for Men & Women

"In trying to successfully build a medically-based spa in an increasingly-competitive environment, I've been looking for a useful source of information – and I've found it in Cheryl Whitman's new book, Beautifully Profitable. Her guidelines on staging promotional events, beginning with event planning – including practical check-lists – as well as her insights into cost-saving internal marketing ideas, was particularly helpful. Strongly recommended for spa owners and managers who intend to succeed in 2014 and beyond."

Dr. Marcy Street, Doctor's Approach Dermatology & Laser Center, Cosmetic Surgery & Med-Spa, and creator of Doctor's Approach Skin and Hair Care, Okemos Michigan

"Too many aesthetic and cosmetic physicians and surgeons in private practice tend to forget that, in addition to treating patients, they are running a retail business offering services and products. For them, Cheryl Whitman's newest book, Beautifully Profitable, will serve an invaluable tool. Through the pages of this book, she guides physicians through the basics of business and marketing, before offering them a road-map to new profit centers, as well as clearly describing practice-building techniques. Highly recommended for every doctor – not just in the aesthetics field – who is in private practice."

Dr. Robert Bergen, MD, Founder, Retina Associates of New Jersey

"I know that social networking and managing patient testimonials is supposed to be vital to my practice growth, but not only didn't I have the time, but I didn't have a clue about how to successful manage this strange new world. With a new cosmetic center opening soon in VA I found my answers in Beautifully Profitable – and I will be implementing those answers beginning today. Working with Cheryl has helped guide me on the right paths to success."

Dr. Soheila Rostami, MD, Cosmetic Surgeon, Eye Specialist,
Reston Virginia, Washington DC Metro Area

"What do you think is the most visited page of every plastic surgeon's website whose Analytics I've seen? Do you realize just how very important having a pristine gallery is in your overall marketing plan? Think about it. To viewers, quantity and quality is an indication of how successful the practice is. It's time to be brutally honest and take a good look at your gallery, both on your website and how you present them during the consultation. Cheryl Whitman's new book will help you make these assessments, and so much more."

Candace Crowe,
Candace Crowe Design

"I've been looking for a useful source of information – and I've found it in Cheryl Whitman's new book, Beautifully Profitable. Her team has guided us with successful events – including practical day to day invaluable advice. They were very hands on and practical I was also drawn to their in-depth expert insights into products, branding and private labeling. Strongly recommended for physicians and practice managers who intend to succeed and keep on top of what's going on in the aesthetic & wellness industry. I have found Cheryl and her team to be sensitive, knowledgeable and current on all of our industries advancements. Our professional relationship has also grown into a beautiful friendship."

Geri Greaney, Practice Manager, Dr. Victoria Karlinsky, New Look, New Life – New York City

Table of Contents

Introduction

A Letter From The Author

This book represents the compilation of practical, valuable and professional experience my team and I at *beautiful forever* (www.beautifulforever.com) have gathered over several decades.

During this time we have helped countless physicians, surgeons, med-spa owners and others create, launch and grow successful aesthetic Medical Practices and related businesses. **This wealth of experience and expertise has provided the solid practical grounding for this book.**

My professional background as an educator has uniquely suited me for the role of not only helping my clients to succeed – *but also teaching them how to succeed!* ***And that is what this book is about – it is a guide to help you learn how to successfully grow your practice or aesthetics business.***

It's my version of "give a man a fish, and he eats for a day; teach a man to fish and he eats for a lifetime."

As part of my continuing commitment to education, I have recently created the *beautiful forever university*, an informational resource, ongoing practice-building education and training tool available to those in the aesthetics industry. The information is also often applicable to any Medical Practice. ***You can learn more about it, and the services my team offers, in the final appendix to this book.***

As both an educator and a practice consultant I have given hundreds of talks and presentations at professional conferences and webinars, and also authored countless articles in professional journals, blogs, white papers, case studies, etc.

I have done this, all while focusing on my primary role; ***helping people successfully manage and market their aesthetic businesses.***

In addition, I have created an eminently practical step-by-step guide and hands-on workbook, *The Aesthetic Medical Success System – A Complete*

Education Guide to Building, Managing and Marketing Your Cosmetic Practice or Medical Spa. Published in 2009, became the only aesthetic educational manual offered by the *American Society of Plastic Surgeons®* to its members.

No longer available from ASPS®, it is still available from **beautiful forever** on our website, (www.beautifulforever.com).

However, most of what we do at **beautiful forever** is guide and support aesthetic and cosmetic physicians and surgeons – as well as med-spa owners and managers – as they dream up and create new businesses. Then we help them launch successfully and, finally, **we continue working with them to help their businesses profitably grow.**

We do it all, from evaluating the nuts-and-bolts of the business side of their endeavors to helping them to market themselves and their operations. **It is the marketing and promotion aspect of the business that is the focus of this book.**

A quick glance at the Table of Contents will demonstrate what this book covers – from strategic planning, to writing a blog or a press release ... and everything in between. Each of the chapters is based on our many years of experience and expertise in successfully assisting doctors and business owners.

The advice we share in this book will be eminently practical to your own business, and from it you will learn how to succeed!

This book is based largely on a compilation of material of recent years that I have created for professional speaking engagements, conferences and webinars and published in a variety of trade and professional journal articles, etc. This material has been edited to provide a strong flow of continuity.

I would like to acknowledge the publishers who graciously returned to me the rights to use and adapt material I had created for their initial use, especially *Inga Hansen at MedEsthetics*, who was also the inspiration for many such articles.

I would also like to acknowledge *Debbie Taylor of TaylorMade Printing Services* as well as *writing and marketing expert Ned Barnett*, who worked on a tight deadline to pull this together. I would also like to thank *my terrific team,* who helped make ***beautiful forever*** the success it is today.

I would like to dedicate this book to my wonderful husband and kids – and especially my parents. Their firm and loving New York upbringing, along with the hard-work-ethic gene they bestowed on me, helped to make me the person I am today. Thank you!

I also want to dedicate this book to my extended family and friends, including *Dr. Janet Brill* – she's been a major inspiration – and all who have put up with my crazy schedule and the demands that come with running a successful business designed to serve the needs of an ever-growing clientele.

Without their love and support, none of this could have happened.

Finally, a portion of the proceeds from the sale of this book will go to *Mazon* – my husband Bob is on the board of this remarkable Jewish charity that feeds the hungry of all faiths. And, from the proceeds, we'll also make a donation to the SIDS Foundation in loving memory of our grandson, "AJ" Andrew Marrara.

Cheryl Whitman
January, 2015

New Profit Center Opportunities

2015 and Beyond

The following are a list of profit centers that will become more significant in 2015 and beyond.

These can bring new revenue and new profit to your medical practice, especially if you first determine if there is a market for those new services that your practice can capitalize on, then if you also make contact with experts who can smooth the path to integrating new and profitable services into your practice.

Each of these are offered in brief bullet-point form, and can serve as a reference or a check-list for Medical Practices or spas that are considering where and how to expand in 2015 and beyond.

Many of these profit centers are covered in significant detail within this book, and you can learn more about any of them, and how they might work in your practice, by contacting me at *beautiful forever*.

Before getting to the profit centers, however, it might be useful to consider some trends identified by the American Society of Plastic Surgeons in their 2013 Plastic Surgery Statistics Support, available on their website.

In a one-year trend, from 2012 to 2013

Number	Procedures	Trend
15.1 mil.	Cosmetic procedures	Up 3%
1.6 mil.	Cosmetic surgical procedures	Up 1%
13.5 mil.	Cosmetic minimally-invasive procedures	Up 3%
5.7 mil.	Reconstructive procedures	Up 2%

The Top Five Cosmetic Surgical Procedures of 2013 vs. 2012

Number	Procedures	Trend
290,000	Breast Augmentation	Up 1%
221,000	Nose Reshaping	Down 9%
216,000	Eyelid Surgery	Up 6%
200,000	Liposuction	Down 1%
133,000	Facelift	Up 6%

Other trending surgeries include Male breast reduction (up 11%), Hair Transplantation (down 8%) and Upper Arm Lifts (up 2%).

2013 Top Five Cosmetic Minimally-Invasive Procedures vs. 2012

Number	Procedures	Trend
6.3 mil.	Botulinum toxin	Up 3%
2.2 mil.	Soft Tissue Filler	Up 13%
1.2 mil.	Chemical Peel	Up 3%
1.1 mil.	Laser Hair Removal	Down 4%
970,000	Microdermabrasion	No Change

2013 Top Five Reconstructive Procedures vs. 2012

Number	Procedures	Trend
4.4 mil.	Tumor Removal	Up 5%
254,000	Laceration Repair	Down 13%
199,000	Maxillofacial Surgery	Down 5%
177,000	Scar Revision	Up 4%
131,000	Hand Surgery	Up 6%

Those are the major one-year trends in plastic surgery in 2013, the last year for which statistics are available.

What isn't noted in this study is the dramatic increase in the number of medical doctors, such as OB/GYN and ENT physicians, who are adding cosmetic treatments to their services, even though they specialize in some other kinds of procedures.

This is part of a larger trend of physicians *"fleeing"* from insurance-covered and Medicare/Medicaid-covered care because of down-trending reimbursement and up-trending paperwork and regulations. This trend is expected to accelerate, making the market far more competitive for cosmetic physicians and surgeons.

This accelerating trend makes creating and promoting profitable programs all the more important for your practice, and for your future.

Answers to some fundamental questions can be enlightening. They can also provide the point of departure as you take your Medical Practice to the next level, by adding new profit centers.

- For instance, are employees properly trained on all procedures and equipment?

- Are you in compliance with state laws and regulations?

- Does your information technology adequately support the Medical Practice?

- Is the website up to date?

- Are your business and marketing plans current?

- What about the staff compensation plan and budget?

If you are considering adding new aesthetic services, skincare products, or any other products or services, you will also need to answer a series of operational questions in order to form your plan.

For example:

- Which product and service offerings are most needed in my service area?

- Which services will bring the most clients through the door—and keep them coming back?

- Which will be most profitable to deliver?

- What is the level of investment needed to get started?

- What equipment do I need for the procedures? How do I choose which vendor to use?

- Should I buy or lease?

- Are my current state licenses and insurance coverage sufficient for the new product/service offerings?

- Will I need to hire new staff or provide training for the new product/service area?

- Will staff compensation plans change?

- How do I establish a pricing structure for the new services? Will new financing options be needed for my clients?

In taking advantage of many of these new profit-center opportunities, there is an easy way and a hard way – a way that capitalizes on practical experience, and a way that gives you that practical experience.

If you or a staff member has expertise in a given area – as well as the spare time to make use of that expertise – you can probably manage adding these new services yourself.

However, if time is short or expertise is lacking, it is both prudent and profitable to capitalize on the knowledge of existing experts, rather than becoming an expert yourself.

Now, here are these emerging profit centers.

Patient Financing Programs

- Patient financing programs will help physicians offer services to their patients

- Financing is now available for patients whose credit scores are as low as 550

- Medical Practices can create custom programs for their clients, such as 6 months interest free, etc., to improve their competitive edge

Marketing and Cash Services

- Physicians and spas are starting to install cash programs in many offices – there are regulations here regarding the presence of a physician, so be sure to check with your consultants, accountants and others before implementing this type of program

- The four main areas of focus are:

    o Bio-identical Hormone Replacement Therapy

    o Weight Management Programs

    o Aesthetics such as Botox and fillers

    o Regenerative Therapies such as PRP

Ongoing practice marketing

Physicians and spas are increasingly taking a combined qualitative and quantitative approach to their marketing programs with the goal of developing an efficient and effective marketing plan that comprises a reasonable percent of your revenue, and has ROI measurements so it more than pays for itself.

These approaches are detailed in this book.

Private Label Product Development

As an extension of a practice or spa's brand – as well as an additional revenue stream – private label skin care products are becoming increasingly important in the market. ***This book lays out what is required to set up a private label line that meets or surpasses brand name lines, as well as the pluses and minuses.***

We will direct you to the right manufacturers to meet your expectations and the best product line for your projected volume and budget.

Be assured that your private label line can become a reality with a minimum investment and there are no large minimums required. Additional savings can be realized by using your private label line in your back bar and treatment room.

Product lines vary in cost, as well as the length of time it takes to complete the manufacturing process. There are several options based on your budget.

- **Option 1**: Use Consultants to source 6-8 "private label" stock products based on your input and create a new logo and graphic design to be used on the chosen vendors bottles or jars. This is both a great and an easy way to start selling skincare products with your own brand name.

- **Option 2**: Professional product creation and packaging experts will source 10-12 "private label" stock products based on your input and create a new logo and graphic design to be used on the chosen vendors bottles or jars. This Option also includes creating the concept and design and for a "Kit" or regimen package. This is a significantly more comprehensive approach than Option 1, and is also a great way to start selling skincare products with your own brand name.

- **Option 3**: The Platinum Design Package – This Option includes everything described in Option 2, and also includes the design for a brochure or menu of services up to 6 pages, shelf talkers for each product describing the product attributes and helps to "sell" products to the patient. Also includes sourcing and applying your new logo artwork to a shopping bag style of your choosing.

PR – Publicity, Promotion and Media Relations

Medical Practices and spas are increasingly seeing the need for new and effective promotion efforts, and are turning to public relations – making use of opportunities to tell their stories through the news media – in addition to social networking to get the message out. ***Both are covered in this book.***

Typically, professional public relations includes:

- Identifying, contacting and working with members of the news media to bring favorable attention to you and your practice.

- Integrated image-building, brand-building and patient-educational publicity programs designed to gain awareness for physician and practice

- Programs that position the practice leader as an expert in his or her field, and get the news media calling for more information related to breaking news stories

- Customized or standardized news media relations tools designed and implemented, over time, to connect the doctor (or other client) with the media as *the* (and *their*) expert in a specific field

- Develop a calendar of planned future press outreach efforts, to ensure ongoing progress and growth of the client as a perceived expert

- Create press releases designed to generate favorable press coverage, and present them to the news media in a way that attracts their favorable attention

Marketing

Medical Practices and spas are increasingly creating or enhancing physician marketing and promotional efforts in an efficient fashion. These innovative programs – ***many addressed in this book*** – are designed to support efforts to increase physician brand image and practice awareness.

They do this through effective marketplace positioning, enhanced brand recognition and marketing-generated prospect interest.

These programs, along with practice management programs, are being designed to improve client conversion rates, increase the rate of patient up-sells with product development and enhance overall operations and efficiency of staff.

Staff Training

This high-level effort is increasingly significant as the marketplace becomes more competitive. Medical Practices are bringing in management and training experts who are skilled at working with physicians and practice staffs. Some do this via remote programs, often in conjunction with periodic on-site visits. These are all designed to improve operations, enhance conversions and support up-selling, cross selling and improved sales, and they are *all covered extensively in this book.*

Events

Events bring people to the Medical Practice office, the spa, or to hear the physician. These events are increasingly significant as practice-building marketing tools.

This is covered extensively in this book, and there are checklists in the Appendix you can use to help you implement them.

Before you schedule your event, stop and think about its main purpose.

Identify your goal for the event first. This will help guide your decisions in planning the event. *Are you hosting the event to thank your existing patients, or to attract new ones? Are you launching a new treatment or product and want to create a buzz among a specific target audience, or are you just trying to build marketplace awareness of your brand and your Medical Practice?*

Working with your brand and budget, as well as with your desired outcome, you should strive to create an experience that your attendees will remember. In addition to showcasing your products and services, the event should also differentiate your Medical Practice from those of your competition in a positive manner.

Mystery Shopping and Mystery Calls

The basic "mystery shopping" process involves having a trained professional mystery shopper call, ask questions, and then make an appointment.

A more in-depth and useful "mystery shopper" involves having that same "mystery shopper" actually come in and experience a preliminary assessment.

Either way, that professional then completes a detailed Mystery Shopping Checklist, and follows that up with a detailed report.

Samples are included in the Appendix.

Medical Practice Evaluations

As the market becomes ever more complex, savvy physicians and spa managers are turning to outside professionals for insights into their businesses that will lead to greater profitability.

It is a challenge to treat patients or manage a Medical Practice day-to-day, and still have the high-level skills to conduct any of the following kinds of analyses:

- Cost structure analysis

- Database analysis / review

- Discussions physician(s)

- Interior design & retail space analysis

- Interviews with staff

- Location & signage evaluation

- Marketing review, including budgets, collateral materials & public relations

- Profit & Loss (P&L) analysis

- Product line evaluation

- Technology assessment

- Implementation

- Review of menu of services

- Website & search engine marketing review

- Post-assessment written report & conference call

Hair Transplant Consulting/Medical Practice Overview

Physicians, surgeons, medical spas, medical aesthetic practices, cosmetic surgeons and related entities are all starting to evaluate their ability to develop a highly-profitable hair transplant practice within their existing centers. This is often part of an effort to expand their locations, or to grow their existing hair transplant practice and volume. For most aesthetic physicians, this opens the door to a new market they would otherwise not see.

In most cases, professional consulting services are needed to make this evaluation, and should include – but are not limited to:

- Medical Practice Assessment

- Market assessment/feasibility

- Staff assessment

- Brand development

- Medical Practice set up

- Recruitment of medical/surgical assistants

- Training of medical/surgical assistants

- Physician/surgeon training for conventional strip, FUE and other techniques

- Evaluate new technologies in hair restoration, including Neografting, laser, robotics, microscope, etc.

- Development of pricing, physician and staff compensation, incentive programs, etc.

- Marketing strategy, planning and execution

- Development of web site, micro site and social media presence for hair restoration service

- Internal staff and sales training, including telemarketing (inbound & outbound), in-office sales consultations, web/Skype consultations, webinars, etc. *(note, the new Google Hangouts tool may provide a superior platform for Skype consultations, especially once it has received market acceptance – a tool to keep your eye on)*

- Development of training manuals and sales consultation material for the office

- Develop brochures, posters, inserts, email blasts, press releases, and write-ups for hair restoration

- Developing a network and strategic alliances in the hair restoration professional community

- Development of data metrics, financial metrics, financial analysis of hair business including P&L and ROI

- Develop a product line for hair restoration solutions for both men and women

- Develop women's hair transplant services including eyebrow, eyelash, front hair line, etc.

- Develop ancillary men's hair transplant services (e.g. beard, mustache, eyebrow, body hair, etc.)

- Explore international opportunities for hair restoration income

- Ongoing business, marketing, clinical and ancillary support to make the hair restoration business successful, profitable and sustainable.

From my team's extensive experience and expertise – more than ten years of developing and managing in the U.S. and overseas, I can testify to the huge potential for profit, and the need to bring in professionals who understand this market.

Conclusion to the Introduction

The aesthetics market is booming – not only are more Americans using these services than ever before, but more physicians are entering the field as they attempt to flee from insurance-driven and often profitless Medical Practice, into a field of elective and often cash-pay services. This means more customers yet much more competition.

Those who succeed in the face of this competition will be those who prepare for the battle of the marketplace!

Marketing is a kind of economic warfare – for any given patient, there is only one winner, but there could be several losers. Its zero-sum competition – patients *"do not spread it around"* to several practitioners.

This book will show you how to master many of the most important marketing warfare techniques and tactics, to help make sure that you – and not your competitor down the hall or across the street – will get that patient's business.

Chapter One: Building a Retail Business

Building a retail business is a tremendous challenge, one that many physicians and surgeons find themselves ill-prepared to tackle. Medical school is not business school, and working for another doctor's Medical Practice offers little hands-on-training for running your own Medical Practice.

And whatever else it may be, an aesthetics Medical Practice, with or without an add-on med-spa, is a retail business, one that offers clients retail services, with no insurance interference or negotiations, as well as products, including private-label products.

This is what this book is all about. Building a Medical Practice or a med-spa – one that becomes a profitable and rewarding retail business while demonstrating both the passion and professionalism of the doctor or owner - that is the challenge this book accepts.

Each subject is designed to help the reader undertake one aspect of building a successful business. The book is designed to be read, start-to-finish, for those who want a full grounding in the subject matter – but it's also sectioned off so the reader can go directly to what information he or she needs at any given moment. *Use it as a guide to help you build your business.*

Section One: Marketing and Promoting a Medical Practice

Marketing and promoting a Medical Practice is what most of this book is all about.

To market and promote effectively, you need the following:

- A clear vision of what you want your business to become – as well as a recognition that it is now more than a Medical Practice ... it is also now a Retail Business

- A clear understanding of your target market – whether you call them clients, patients or guests, they are your source of revenue

- A clear understanding of what the members of your target market want from a service like yours

- A clear grasp of the competition, and of the competitive landscape

- A clear understanding of the communications media you plan to use

- A practical timeline and an ample budget

- A commitment to stay the course and succeed

When you have all of these in place, you are ready to begin your promotion and marketing. Efforts should include the following:

- Bringing back former clients, patients or guests (we'll call them clients here) – once you have made the initial sale, follow-ups are typically much easier

- Encourage current clients to become more frequent clients by offering them appropriate new services or products

- Generate referrals from current and former clients, and reward them for this effort – it is called "referral-development," and it is a very powerful marketing and promotion tool

- Turn your staff into incentivized sales reps, encouraging them to up-sell services and branded products

- Create strategic alliances with other physicians, and with local businesses who serve (but do not compete for) your target audiences – large OB/GYN practices are particularly fruitful. Educate their staffs, offer them incentives and discounts, and in other ways engage these sources for referrals.

- You can do the same kind of training/socializing motivating with hairdressers and others in the fringes of the beauty business. Remember "what's in it for me" and find creative and legal ways of incentivizing these people motivated and happy referral sources.

- Use communications professionals to handle your (ghost) writing and social network postings, PR and advertising – even if you think you have the skills, your time can be used more effectively and profitably

- Use regular communication – emails, newsletters, postal mailings and social networking – to stay in touch with clients and former clients, motivating them to participate again, and to refer others – for this, you need to collect all clients' emails, as well as the emails of prospects

- Use both "Content" (blogs, white papers, webinars, etc.) and "Conversation" (personal-sounding posts) on social networking sites to maintain contact and attract new followers who can be converted into clients or patients

- Build up "content" over time then edit it into an eBook that can be used as an incentive and add to your credibility

- Use press releases to support and enhance social networking to reach new targets – go beyond just reporting on new services in your Medical Practice – use your professional expertise to comment on the bad treatments celebrities received right before the Academy Awards (for instance), or in other ways tie into what is going on in the world around you

- Use advertising selectively, carefully – key words on Google can work, but test them – and local advertising should be created by a professional (not by the media) and an ad-placement plan created by that professional (again, not by the media, who have their own incentives not your best interests)

- Be consistent – promotion takes time and intensity and consistency – what advertisers call "reach and frequency" – to be effective, so allow enough time and enough budget to reach success ... every now and then you can catch "lightning in a bottle," but plan on earning success the hard way, and you will be sure of that success

Follow these steps, using these tools – and the more practical and detailed steps found in this book, and you will find success!

Back to Basics

Can You Answer These Questions About Your Medical Practice?

Introduction

A successful aesthetic Medical Practice must not only exhibit professional skills and expertise, but must be able to establish and maintain a good rapport with all its colleagues and patients.

Aesthetic medicine is no longer a trend – it is an industry staple, one that offers physicians a way to create a complimentary and profitable business model.

Today, Managed Care (dare I say "mis-managed care?") and government mandates about insurance, finds clerks and government bureaucrats are telling doctors how they can practice. That is a major reason why aesthetics medicine – which is predominantly self-pay – can work outside those imposing intrusions into your practice of medicine.

This is attracting more professionals from insurance-based practices to cash-based practices – for those, this book can be remarkably helpful.

This chapter's section focuses on taking the necessary steps to cover the business basics in establishing, maintaining and growing your retail business and is essential in developing a successful medical spa.

Do you have what it takes?

Staying ahead of the "power curve" and developing a can-do and will-do attitude – staying the course no matter what may try to derail you – is the essential character-defining attribute of the successful aesthetic medical entrepreneur.

Before you branch out into aesthetics medicine, ask yourself:

- Do you have what it takes to be a leader in this ultra-hot market space?

- Are you ready to expand your Medical Practice service offerings and provide your patients with services they are currently seeking from other sources?

Before you start, conduct a rigorously-honest self-assessment – see if now the time is for you. Ask:

- Is funding in place, or has it at least been identified?

- Remember what Donald Trump said about successful real estate – "location, location, location – then realize that this applies to you. You cannot succeed with a carriage-trade Medical Practice from the depths of Hell's Kitchen or Fort Apache – The Bronx. So, do you have the right location?

- Do you want a professional building vs. a retail space? Hint: If you're going upscale and self-pay, retail is probably NOT the way to go.

- Do you know what marketing efforts it will take to get people through your door?

As consultants, not a day goes by when we don't see a doctor making penny-wise and pound-foolish decisions about the signage and build out costs being added to their leases as they try to expand into aesthetics medicine. If you're going there, you need experienced professional guidance, and you need to listen to your savvy marketer.

- Finally, do you have your concept? Is there something that sets you apart, something that will attract qualified patients? If so, find it and capitalize on it. If not, reconsider your move into aesthetics. To succeed, you have to stand out.

Do you know your target audience?

Your concept – that special something which defines you and your Medical Practice – is, on the bottom line, both who you are and what you are offering to your clients.

Ask yourself: "What's one thing I can say I am an expert in?"

Your concept cannot just be that as an "aesthetic practice." One of the greatest pitfalls of any business – and especially in aesthetics – is trying to be "everything to everybody."

You need to concentrate in areas that complement your Medical Practice. When you offer too many choices, trying to cover too many services, you ultimately just confuse the patient while reducing your potential profitability.

Create a service menu compatible with your Medical Practice, offering competitive prices – which is essential at the start.

Your ultimate goal is to create – in the public's mind – a solid concept of who you are and what your aesthetics Medical Practice is – a concept that maintains your integrity while being marketable. With this, you will generate revenue, position yourself for growth and encourage loyalty.

Budget and Allocation

Because advertising will likely be the most expensive part of your marketing budget, how much you invest in advertising and other marketing initiatives, as well as how it is allocated, should be researched carefully. Whenever possible, find the lowest-cost alternative that works.

Think outside the box. Don't do what your competition is doing. Consider actually go in the other direction and create new services and packages they don't offer.

Creating an overlap of services is acceptable, but work hard to create unique solutions to unmet market needs. See what patients are looking for, create surveys and run local focus groups with different ages and ask what they need.

Differentiating yourself from the rest of the market will help you grow your Medical Practice, increase your revenues, maintain your fair share of the market, attract a better patient and beat your competition. Successful marketing tactics involve external and internal marketing methods as well as creative and innovative thinking.

Internal

Be sure your office ambience is inviting, comfortable and is a representation of you. If you have not updated your Medical Practice in quite a while, it is time to redecorate with new colors and textures. Include soft lighting, music and art to portray your aesthetic interest.

Display your credentials, testimonials and photo albums; this is also a good place to show off your work.

Be sure your staff is friendly, professional and caring to every patient, every time. *Nothing is more important than patient relations, and a great staff is crucial to your success.*

In addition, look at your patients' experiences from their point of view. Be sure there is a smooth transition from each step in the patient flow process. It takes training and conscientiousness on everyone's part to make this smooth and effortless.

Finally, "internal marketing" – be it wall-posters or a well-trained and incentivized staff who focus on sales, or even email marketing to existing and former patients – this is often the most cost-effective, and least costly, form of marketing. Begin with this foundation, and you're well on your way to success.

External

The focus of external marketing is reaching out to your potential patients, so analyze your local market and determine what will connect with your target market most effectively.

To ensure your message is on target, review your current efforts. Be sure it portrays you as the expert in your field and the No. 1 choice for them.

Have your Web site address printed on everything so people can easily find you on the Internet. All of these tools help, when done properly they will help the image you are trying to portray. Be sure they are top quality, positioning you as the industry expert who knows the latest technology and procedures.

Getting involved in your community can give you tremendous exposure. Every community has its "movers and shakers," so get to know them by attending their events and offering to speak. Get involved in local charities and fundraising events. There is great PR in being seen as caring and committed to your community.

In the meantime start with your current patient base. They already know and trust you. Implement some "fast-acting" marketing projects that give you revenues now such as:

- Direct Mail

- Newsletter

- Internet Marketing

- Gift Certificates

- VIP Cards

- Word-of-mouth Referral Program

- In-House Events

Tracking Results

To measure your marketing success, you must effectively and consistently track your new patients and prospects. You do this to find out how your new patients are finding their ways to your office.

The easiest way to track results is a log near the telephones to remind the receptionist to ask. She can then enter that information into a software program.

You will be able to pull up reports to track trends and marketing results.

Do you have a plan?

An updated documented plan is the backbone of your project. A business plan is an important first step in making your business a success. You can dramatically increase your odds for success by going through the process of creating a focused business plan.

It is never too late to create a business plan. It is great if you create one as part of the business start up as a good first step in a solid foundation. Whether you are looking to expand, entice an investor or if you are funding the project yourself, a written plan of action is essential.

It gives everyone who reads it a thorough understanding of your vision. It is here that you will verbalize your theme, concept and business goals.

A good business plan needs to address a variety of important topics, including:

Income and Revenue: Think about all of the possible income streams from services, procedures, and retail. The medical spa business is built on small margins and if you are not selling a lot of products, the margins are even thinner.

Expenses: Determine accurate figures related to expenses for labor, workman's compensation, taxes and benefits, cost of goods, rent, etc. Some Medical Practices report their labor cost alone often exceeds 50 percent of their total revenue.

Profit and Loss Statement: Setting realistic profitability expectations is essential to the success of this project. It is important to set realistic goals and revenue projections in order to complete a break even analysis.

Construction and Setup: Diligent business planning requires careful examination of such items as architecture and design, construction costs, furniture and fixtures, equipment, uniforms, initial retail inventory, linen, training, and marketing.

Be well informed and updated on all your insurance needs, compliance issues and training. Know your state laws, they are changing and getting tougher all the time. Set yourself up from the beginning with all of this in mind.

Do you know your costs?

Direct costs are associated with the delivery of patient care.

Indirect costs, or overhead costs, are not connected with the production of goods or services. However, they are an important component of running your business.

Industry standards suggest that overhead costs should represent between 45% and 60% of your total operating costs, depending on your specialty and the services you provide.

If your overhead costs are outside the recommended range, carefully analyze each overhead item and take corrective action. Not only do you need good financial planning/budgeting, revenue cycle management, and control of your overhead expenses. You also need internal control systems that help you manage the cash in your Medical Practice.

Many physicians have become complacent with regard to financial oversight. They have relied too heavily upon others to manage their financial affairs.

The reality of the situation is that no one has a higher interest level in your finances than you. Getting the right information is critical to making better decisions about your business.

Create a budget

Having a plan and a budget with operational and expenditure parameters is essential to successful daily operations. A budget is simply a financial planning tool that lists all planned expenses and revenues. It is a forecasting tool which enables the management team to apply appropriate intervention in a timely manner.

Make sure that you diligently work within the parameters of your budget. When you exceed the budget, strive to understand what happened. Have your management team provide the cause and avoid going over budget in the future. Holding yourself and your team accountable is essential to the success of budgetary compliance.

Do you have the right team in place?

One of the most important parts of an aesthetic Medical Practice is your staff. Without a strong staff, your day can be miserable. The smart physicians will surround themselves with exceptional staff so that they can "delegate tasks to these competent staff to carry out the practice's plans.

Most of the procedures found in an aesthetic Medical Practice are perfect for medical aestheticians and nurses to perform.

In most medical offices, you'll find a practice manager who handles the day to day business of running an office so that the physician is free to care for patients. Having a practice manager is especially important for aesthetic physicians who need assistance in not only running an office but in marketing and advertising.

Aesthetic medicine is a business, and physicians normally don't have the education or wherewithal to handle both their patient load and the operational issues that most Medical Practices have today. Critical members of your team will include outside professional experts – your accountant, your attorney, and your practice consultant.

All of these should be integrated into your team – the more they know about your operation and goals, the more likely they are to be able to help.

It is also important to remember that in order to have a successful aesthetic Medical Practice you should make great service a priority.

Excellent customer service requires training your staff and constantly reinforcing the message that patient satisfaction comes first.

Be sure they're properly trained on your procedures, credentials and patient relations. Hold regular staff meetings so everyone is on the same page, and offer them complementary procedures so they can relay first-hand experience to your patients.

Of course, don't forget your receptionist.

They are the first contact your patient will have with your Medical Practice, and first impressions are very important!

Give your patients a quality experience and complete satisfaction, and they'll keep coming back for more.

Do you know your competition?

Knowing your competition inside and out is essential to ensure that you do not create a medical spa that has to take business away from potential competitors.

Instead, you want to carve out your own unique niche that may attract an untapped market for your special services.

Be sure to check out the competition thoroughly. How? One way to learn about the competition is to first identify them and then visit their operation. Make an appointment and see what they offer.

Visit their websites. Look at staff credentials, number of staff members, services offered, and fees charged. Make extensive phone calls to gather menus of everything offered in the area.

Once you have checked out the competition, you will know what services they offer. To be successful, provide alternative services – give the public what it is currently lacking.

Are you up to date on all of the latest procedures and treatments?

There are several strategies to keep the economics of an aesthetic Medical Practice in balance: you can work more hours and see more patients; raise fees; cut costs further; OR offer new, up-to date cash-based services.

RealSelf's Consumer Cosmetic Treatment Survey, conducted by Harris Interactive, reported that, "if money were not an issue," 69% of adults would seek out minimally invasive procedures. This was an increase over 2009 reports, by 14%.

Of the treatments that adults would entertain, teeth whitening was at the top of the list (48%), followed by hair removal (27%), cellulite treatments (14%), vein treatments (13%), dermal filler procedures (12%), laser skin treatments (9%), chemical peels and botox (7%).

Stay up-to-date on all the latest medical procedures and treatments for a variety of conditions within expertise. Develop your Medical Practice to include the newest treatments and widen your scope of aesthetic services to include any areas you feel comfortable exploring in order to provide good service to as many patients as possible.

Don't forget that knowing your competition will allow you to see what is lacking in your area and allow you to focus on those missing services. Your Medical Practice should seem more concerned with the patient's health than making money.

You can also sell more large packages and service series in advance.

Are you making the most out of your "retail business"?

Global sales of physician-dispensed cosmeceuticals reached $774.9 million in 2008 – an increase of 13.4% in just one year. Through 2012, growth of this segment is projected at up to 17.1% per year as physicians continue adding skincare lines to augment their aesthetic treatment services.

The last thing anyone should do is sit tight through a slow economy and watch the recession attack their bottom line. Consumers continue to spend billions of dollars each year on anti-aging skincare products and implementing these products into your Medical Practice can increase total revenues by as much as 40%. Anti-aging skincare products can achieve great results for your patients' skin as well as your Medical Practice.

Anti-aging products are the leading category within the U.S. skincare market, and in 2010 they account for 60% of overall Cosmeceutical product demand. By 2011, the U.S. population over age 50 will increase by 56%. This group's collective spending power currently exceeds $900 billion per year, which is a healthy indicator, as well as a good reason to consider adding anti-aging skincare to your Medical Practice in the near future.

If you are ready for the adventure, consider launching a custom skincare line all your own. A well-developed private label skincare line extends your patients' visits by providing personalized products they can use at home. The process of creating a private label skincare line is less complex than you might think and the benefits are plentiful.

A custom skincare product line can be extremely lucrative, adding between 30% and 40% to your total revenues. The mark-up on private label products can be as much as 300%, depending on the types of products you choose.

Your business Consultant who knows the aesthetic business is an important piece of your development team from beginning to end of your project. A consultant team that has years of business experience will sharpen your concept, create your menus, recommend products and equipment, make sure your facility is functional and your concept is consistent throughout its design.

They will implement your infrastructure, teach you how to recruit, hire and train your staff and help you to open the doors and begin generating revenue.

This will help you avoid costly mistakes and generate real and measurable success.

Section Two: Medical Practice Marketing Metrics

Measuring a business or Medical Practice – and measuring the impact of your marketing, are essential to success.

The following will help to make measuring a bit clearer.

Financial Metrics
Your Balance Sheet for Success

Don't let your numbers sneak up on you. Organizations that rely on solid numbers and key metrics, rather than subjective measures such as hearsay and intuition, have the edge on financial success. Learn how financial metrics can be used to manage your business and help determine how your services and products can better grow your business and build its financial success.

Discover important measurements to include so you can get a good handle on your numbers and ensure that your dollars are being spent efficiently and effectively. To adequately measure your financial metrics, discuss this with your accountant or business manager, and set up a means of screening revenue sources on a regular basis.

Client and Consultation Metrics
Measurements for success

Satisfied customers are the key to your spa's profitability, so measuring your customers' satisfaction on a regular basis is vital. Learn how to identify the measurements you should focus on so you can provide your team with the information they need to excel, while determining which approaches cause you to fall below your goals and which exceed expectations and bear repeating.

Get feedback that provides vital coaching opportunities to help your team build essential skills, increase industry knowledge and enhance customer service skills to encourage client loyalty and increase client retention.

Demographic and Lead Metrics Measurements for Success

Want to increase your market share and revenue? Wondering how you can grow beyond your current client base? Demographic and lead metrics play a key role in determining just how large your target market is.

Learn how these vital measurements can help you pinpoint growth opportunities, as well as recognize obstacles that can hamper your success.

With the added benefit of best Medical Practices, learn how to identify the prospects you absolutely want to see, as well as a new target audience you have not previously recognized. Understanding your data will give you with a powerful, competitive tool that can help identify the demographics of your target market and determine the best lead generation avenues.

Performance Metrics
The SMART Way to Make Business Measurements Work for You

Performance, or business, metrics measure what is happening in your Medical Practice at any given time. This attention to detail can help turn your mission statement into goals that can be clearly demonstrated, monitored and evaluated.

Learn how these external measures are connected to outputs, customer needs and business requirements to make it all happen. Build the skills you need to gather information and detect trends that will get true measurements of performance for the purpose of overall improvement – something that will benefit your entire organization.

Also, included is the SMART metrics method that will help you develop measurements that are **S**pecific, **M**easurable, **A**ctionable, **R**elevant, and **T**imely.

Marketing Metrics
Getting the Most from Your Marketing Dollars

You know you need to market, but how effective are your methods? The goal of marketing metrics is to give you the best information to make wisest investment decisions.

Learn how to measure the impact of your efforts, refine and optimize your "marketing mix" to capture more, use "market basket analysis" for deeper saturation and make the most of your existing customer base and the emerging prospect market. You measure your marketing by tracking where your patients come from.

If they respond to email, you know it's working, and valuable. If they don't come from TV ads, you know they're a waste of money, and need to be revamped. There are very useful and cost-effective tracking tools available that I work with, and refer them to my clients.

Discover the information you need to gather to determine how well your marketing dollars are currently working. By regularly taking the pulse of your marketing expenditures and programs, you can better manage the process and isolate inefficiencies as they arise.

Section Three: Business Plans

Creating an Individualized Business Plan

The Right Tools for the Job

A business plan is essential to the success of your medical spa or cosmetic Medical Practice. It is the blueprint that will guide your business, as well as defining its structure, services, products, staffing, resources, budgeting, financial management and implementation.

Whether you are seeking start-up or expansion capital, or you're working to keep your investment strong, a solid business plan is a vital element of your financial package. It also has great operational value, especially if it is reviewed and updated quarterly – in this case, it will help to keep your business on track.

A professionally structured plan can help you raise equity, control debt ratios, assess liquidity and raise your business and organization to the next level.

The Expertise You Need

Creating business plans is not part of your Medical School 101 curriculum – but it is essential as you transition your Medical Practice into something more – a profitable retail business.

To create a successful and effective business plan, use a professional planner who understands the cosmetic and aesthetic business, as well as the fine art of strategic planning. Their sharply honed skills in preparing solid business plans that get results are essential to success. Such experts have helped many clients secure the funding they need, on many occasions within days, by helping them prepare reliable business plans that are bank and investor-ready. They can also help practices to use the business plans on an ongoing basis to keep them pointed toward profitability.

Even those clients who do not seek funding can benefit greatly with a focused strategy to help guide the steady, consistent evolution of their businesses over the foreseeable future – both in the short-term and over the long haul.

Look for planners who blend decades of experience with leading-edge software to provide their clients exceptional business plans.

The Next Right Move
Your Marketing Blueprint

Following the development of your business plan, you may opt to create a strategic marketing plan that is focused on your target market. This important tool (addressed in the next section in this chapter) could also be used by your advertising or marketing agency to develop a highly targeted campaign. Take this step to ensure that your marketing dollars are wisely spent for a greater return on investment.

Plan to Succeed

Business plans are vital documents, yet most physicians have little experience even evaluating them. The following list of components will help you to ensure that your business plan is complete and professional.

Your medical practice's strategic business plan will include a combination of elements, such as:

- Executive Summary

- Statement of Assumptions

- Budgeting including Payroll

- Company Overview

- Competitor Assessment

- Corporate, Marketing and Implementation Strategies

- Differentiation and Market Segmentation including Target Market

- Differentiation, Pricing and Promotional Strategies

- Financial and Profitability Analysis

- Financial Projections - Start-up Capital and Operational Expenditures

- Industry Overview including Data

- Management Team, Medical Directors and Team Staffing

- Market Assessment

- Marketing Blueprint

- Menu of Services

- Mission Statement

- Roll-Out Plan

- Product/Retail Strategy

- Project Feasibility

- Regulatory and Legal Considerations

- Risk Assessment

- Working Capital and Break-Even Analysis

- Zip Code Analysis and Mapping

Most business plans are accompanied by a separate set of financial exhibits or spreadsheets delineating:

- Break-even Analysis

- Capital Equipment breakdown

- Three to Five year (annual) Pro Forma P&L

- One year, monthly Pro Forma Profit and Loss (P&L) Statement

- Schedules/Exhibits showing breakdown or assumptions behind specific line items

- Start-up Costs

- Volume assumptions behind financial figures

Section Four: Annual Marketing Plan

Marketing to Budget, Budgeting to Market

I frequently give talks on this critical subject at professional society meetings. This following chapter is distilled from those talks, and from several articles I have published.

Annual marketing plans are useful roadmaps which allow physicians and practice managers to plan ahead, then work that plan throughout the coming year.

A key element in any sound annual marketing plan involves the marketing budget – and to succeed in the coming year, working to budget is just as important as working to plan.

When the marketing plan and the marketing budget are combined, the budget can be measured in terms of return on marketing investment (ROI), ensuring that marketing activities are indeed investments in a more profitable Medical Practice operation.

Before looking at the annual marketing budget – which will be used to define and restrain the marketing efforts to ensure a positive ROI – begin by looking at the elements needed in an annual marketing plan, then determine the budget allocation and potential ROI for each element.

Website – your Medical Practice website has become your single most important marketing and promotion tool. Your website is your "virtual brochure" – the key element in prospective patients' decision to try your Medical Practice.

It is not enough to have a website; you need to have one that is dynamic, ever-evolving representation of the best your Medical Practice has to offer. Your website also becomes your "virtual yellow pages" ad – the primary means by which people who are looking for the right physician or medical spa find you.

You need to have someone in charge who will regularly and frequently update the photos, update the videos, and make the site reflect your practice. It is often helpful to have a skilled consultant evaluate your site from an outside perspective, and help you highlight both opportunities and problems.

Search Engine Optimization (SEO) – with the Internet having effectively and completely replaced traditional yellow pages – long a stalwart of Medical Practice marketing and promotion – it has become essential to rank high in organic searches within your market.

If your Medical Practice website isn't within the first five-to-ten listings, it likely won't be found by people used to accepting the first-page listings as sufficient to their needs.

Marketing-oriented physicians and practice managers have come to realize that, while they may not understand SEO, they know they can't effectively grow their Medical Practices without an effective SEO program.

Search Engine Optimization is a constantly-moving target, as Google continually alters its search parameters to prevent "black hat SEO" hustlers from "gaming" the system. The best ways to win at SEO without being caught "gaming" the system is to play it straight. Include appropriate key words in your writing, and generate legitimate links to your website.

These can occur in wire-placed press releases, posts on blogging sites – including comments you post on others' blogs – as well as social networking posts. These should be including Facebook, LinkedIn, Twitter, YouTube and Google +.

You can also try to work with other online social networks, though these tend to become trendy – then disappear – at an alarming rate. Current favorite up-and-comers include Pinterest and Instagram.

You can also leverage your ranking with integral videos on your sites, and links to and from YouTube postings. If you're going to pursue video social networking on YouTube, set up a free YouTube Network and start logging subscribers. Finally, on all of your websites, blog sites, YouTube postings and wherever else you can, post links that will allow visitors to easily follow you on at least the major social networking sites.

Keyword Advertising – to be successful as a consumer-support business – which is what every self-referral Medical Practice is at its core – Keyword Advertising is critical. However, this is a complex, always-changing practice – to succeed; a Keyword Advertising program requires a professional.

It is not something amateurs can hope to do on their own.

However, done right, Keyword click-through Advertising will channel interested prospects to your website, and from there, to your Medical Practice.

Because Keyword Advertising is so easy to track, it is the single most measurable marketing. Unlike many marketing practices, you will be able to tell at a glance if your key-word investment is generating a positive return on your Medical Practice's marketing investment (ROI).

Social Networking – this marketing promotion approach has evolved, in just the past three-to-five years, from an interesting idea – almost a hobby for practice managers who like to "play" online – to an essential and dynamic marketing tool which has proved to be incredibly effective in attracting patients to your website, and, ultimately, to your Medical Practice.

Social Networking requires two elements in shared priority – content (reasons for people to come to your Facebook page and your website) and conversation (reasons for people to become and stay connected).

Content and Conversation – these take time and effort – but social networking will not succeed without a generous measure of both of these.

To be successful in Social Networking, you need to place useful content online – making use of White Papers and blogs to present that useful content in easily-accessible formats – and you need to be ready to use the most effective tools:

> **Facebook** – several years ago, Facebook eclipsed "MySpace" as the leading online social media community, and Facebook has since attracted somewhere in the neighborhood of a billion users world-wide, including a tremendous number of American adults, who use

it for entertainment, information exchange, friend-building ... and commercial-vendor decision-making.

A presence on Facebook means not only creating a fan page and attracting followers, but it means a sustained commitment to ongoing, regular and frequent outreach to your friends and fans on Facebook via blogs, video blogs and shorter posts, as well as continuing a program of engaging your Facebook friends in dialog, instead of just talking down to them.

Facebook is a complex and ever-changing landscape. Though it seems easy and even obvious, getting the most value out of Facebook requires state-of-the-art experience and up-to-date knowledge of the faster-than-light changes Facebook experience, almost weekly. If you don't have the time to invest in becoming an expert and maintaining that expertise, find a consultant or freelancer who can handle this business-critical function for you.

Twitter – what said about Facebook applies in equal measure to Twitter – except for one fact: the messages must be kept to 140 characters – generally about 20-to-30 words each.

Twitter success requires regular and frequent posts – optimally several times per day – along with a willingness to engage others in conversations, rather than just talking down to them from a position of expertise.

Twitter can be a useful feed to Facebook, as well as to events held at the Medical Practice (or elsewhere); in addition, Twitter has several other useful purposes.

YouTube – Remarkably, YouTube is, after Google, the most prolific search site on the Internet. When people look for information on YouTube, you want to make sure that you are there to be greet them, and to present – in an ongoing series of short (3-5 minute) videos on specific topics of interest – to give them reason to check back with you, to become Facebook Friends and Twitter Followers, and to visit your website (and then your Medical Practice).

Video blogs are useful, but video also allows for compelling testimonials. Video also permits you to record and post information about breaking news in your practice's area of specialization – and it can be fun, critiquing celebrity facelifts (for instance) to present your view on what true enhanced beauty should look like.

YouTube does not require high production values – in fact, too high a production value can turn people off, since it looks scripted instead of spontaneous. Each YouTube post should be promoted on Facebook and Twitter, at least.

Apps: An increasing number of retail businesses – including physician Medical Practices and med-spas, are creating Apps that link consumers to themselves via the consumers' own smart phones. There are an abundance of qualified App developers in the US and especially in India, and the costs for development are no longer out of line with their potential for positive marketing impact.

One of the best things about Social Networking is this: unlike advertising or high-end brochure production, it does not require a significant investment. However, it does require a time commitment.

As a result, frequently, practice managers will retain the services of a ghost writer to produce online content – to be effective, you have to produce useful content on a regular and frequent basis – but beyond that, the costs are nominal.

Events – Special events that bring individuals into the Medical Practice environment are exceptionally effective ways of generating new prospective patients. Events can be tied to calendar themes (Spring "get ready for the beach" events) or other themes (look your best for St. Valentine's Day).

The importance of an Event is that it connects prospects with (and brings back patients to become reconnected with) the physician and the Medical Practice staff. Events can also become fodder for Facebook and Twitter promotions, and can provide videos that can be posted on YouTube.

Public Relations – effective news-media relations programs, when done right, can be remarkably effective in generating awareness and interest, and motivating positive action.

This effectiveness has been compounded by the popularity of the Internet (and Google searches), as well as by the access to the Internet offered by firms such as BusinessWire ensures that every press release is searchable, as are all the media coverage that PR generates.

Public relations, to be effective, requires a professional who understands the fast-changing rules of media relations in the social networking and Internet age. However, because PR is so much more cost-effective than advertising – what you invest in PR is well worth the investment.

Because people have been burned by misleading ads at some time in their lives, advertising tends to have a relatively lower credibility than what you read or see in the news. Advertising is not inexpensive, either – it costs to place ads in the news media, or other locations where prospects will see your message.

However, any story covered by the news media is – according to all the research we've seen – far more credible. People tend to believe what they read in the newspaper or watch on TV news, whereas advertising's message is often dismissed as "just business." As a result, while gaining favorable press coverage takes work – and often a skilled professional practitioner of public relations – the value is all out of proportion to the cost, especially compared to advertising.

For example, an Atlanta-area hospital, which had been running newspaper ads for a new plastic surgery program, caught the eye of CNN. Within two weeks after the coverage, the hospital had 108 new patients who said they heard about it on CNN. The cost for that coverage was essentially zero, and the benefits ran to the hundreds of thousands of dollars. Their advertising was also effective – that was why CNN covered the program – but it was not achieved at zero-cost.

There is room for both. Ads run when you place them, and they say what you want them to say. You control the timing and the message – and the audience – and that is important. PR has higher base credibility, but it is harder to control the message or the timing. When you get it, the benefits are specific.

Finally, PR not only generates new clients, but it supports and reinforces all other marketing and promotion activities.

Direct Marketing: What was once considered a critical promotion tool – direct mail marketing – has been almost entirely replaced by direct email marketing. It is far easier to target – all you need is the right list – and far less costly than direct mail marketing.

However, as is often the case when a new technology replaces the old, when a new approach gets over-used, as is the case with email, physical mail – including hand-written thank-you notes – have even greater impact than they once did. This also works for invitations, announcements of new products, and changes in service mix or location.

The key to successful direct email marketing is an effective list of people who have agreed (opted in) to receive emails from certain sources or on certain topics.

Certainly, the list of Medical Practice patients should be the core of any email marketing campaign; however, refined and focused lists are also available to enable your Medical Practice to reach out beyond current patients and recent prospects.

Advertising: While it is generally the most costly means of marketing, traditional media advertising (newspapers, magazines, radio and TV), advertising continues to be an effective support tool in Medical Practice promotion. The days when advertising is the most important marketing tool are long past, but for some services or products, nothing is more effective than targeted media advertising.

As with public relations and social networking, support from skilled professionals can make all the difference between wasting money and generating a positive marketing/advertising ROI.

Conclusion: Medical Practices grow based on effective marketing. Nothing beats word-of-mouth, but nothing is harder to deliver (on schedule) than effective word-of-mouth. Without being able to count on this, Medical Practices can grow by making use of these marketing tools.

To be successful, create the plan, then apply the budget and pare down the plans to those most likely to generate measurable results. Work the plan, work the budget, then – if you do it right – stand back and watch your Medical Practice grow, generating a positive marketing ROI.

Taking Your Medical Practice to the Next Level
Navigation 101

This section of the chapter is based on a popular talk I give to professional societies and large group Medical Practices, among others ...

Whether you are enjoying busy client traffic in a well established Medical Practice or launching a fledgling enterprise, you need a carefully drawn business and marketing "map" to help you find your way to the next level of success. This valuable tool is something that – like a balance sheet – requires a professional to create, update, and most important, explain to you. Expanding a Medical Practice, adding new products or services, or simply increasing revenues in today's economy requires thoughtful planning and navigation.

Know Your Starting Point

It is surprising how many physicians and business owners are operating without a full awareness of the current state of their Medical Practices. Many say they are too busy delivering services or reacting to day-to-day business problems to stop and apprise what they are doing. This scenario can be risky in volatile economic times.

In many cases, an objective practice assessment from a skilled and experienced professional consultant can provide an objective overview that will spot new revenue sources that have been missed by those too close to the practice to realize what it doesn't have.

Before you begin, it is essential to conduct a basic business and marketing assessment. This process provides a focused view of all aspects of the Medical Practice – costs, revenue, patient scheduling and flow, staff compensation, and much more.

A business assessment helps you to evaluate how well your Medical Practice is currently performing – what's working, what's not, and how you arrived at your current bottom line. And organizations that rely on solid numbers and key metrics, rather than subjective measures such as hearsay and intuition, have the edge on financial success.

Answers to some fundamental questions can be enlightening and provide the point of departure as you take your Medical Practice to the next level.

- For instance, are employees properly trained on all procedures and equipment?

- Are you in compliance with state laws and regulations?

- Does your information technology adequately support the Medical Practice?

- Is the website up to date?

- Are your business and marketing plans current?

- What about the staff compensation plan and budget?

These "living documents" are meant to evolve with the Medical Practice – not sit in a desk drawer – and they should be revisited regularly. They can provide a treasure map to guide any future growth.

Performing even a basic business assessment can be a daunting task, and many physicians use the services of a consultant to provide them with an objective point of view. If you are conducting the assessment yourself, a detailed checklist can be a helpful tool for ensuring that you haven't missed a key variable or metric.

For a free Medical Practice assessment checklist, visit (www.beautifulforever.com).

If you find that the foundation of your Medical Practice is solid, it's probably time to develop a plan to enhance or expand the business.

Explore Your Surroundings

One of the biggest mistakes that physicians and business owners can make is to embark on an expansion or new marketing strategy without examining what the competition is doing. It's vitally important to study the local market and demographics. Knowing what products and services your competitors are currently offering, at what prices, and with what unique benefits to customers, is crucial for a successful expansion.

You may want to assign someone on your staff to gather information on the competition by calling, checking out their websites, and even visiting in person for treatment. Look at staff credentials, number of staff members, and fees. Study the offerings and find out how easy or difficult it is to get an appointment. You can use this information as you develop a plan to create a niche for your Medical Practice or to target a specific segment of the market.

Get Your Bearings

Based on a synthesis of the information you have gained in your business assessment and competitor analysis, you can begin to investigate strategies to grow or expand.

If you are considering adding new aesthetic services or skincare products, you will need to answer a series of operational questions in order to form your plan. For example:

- Which product and service offerings are most needed in my service area?

- Which services will bring the most clients through the door—and keep them coming back?

- Which will be most profitable to deliver?

- What is the level of investment needed to get started?

- What equipment do I need for the procedures? How do I choose which vendor to use?

- Should I buy or lease?

- Are my current state licenses and insurance coverage sufficient for the new product/service offerings?

- Will I need to hire new staff or provide training for the new product/service area?

- Will staff compensation plans change?

- How do I establish a pricing structure for the new services? Will new financing options be needed for my clients?

Chart Your Course

Based on your answers, a direction will begin to take shape and you can create your action plan and budget. The plan that you create should be detailed and somewhat formalized in order to capture the decisions you have made and help you to measure your progress going forward.

If your goal is to maximize revenues from your existing Medical Practice by ramping up sales and marketing efforts, there are lots of new options for taking your Medical Practice to the next level, even in a tight economy.

Keep Moving Forward

Management consultant and self-described "social ecologist" Peter Drucker said, "*The greatest danger in times of turbulence is not the turbulence; it is to act with yesterday's logic.*" Today's logic says that the turbulence of a slowing economy can be endured and even overcome—the key is to keep moving forward.

Section Five: Branding Strategies

Developing and Communicating
Your Personal Brand

Properly managed, your practice's brand is likely to be one of your most valuable assets. A compelling and memorable brand can create the kind of patient loyalty that manifests itself as a preference strong enough to overcome intense competition and price differences.

That level of brand-driven loyalty among patients that can also generate word-of-mouth referrals (and, in this Internet age, "word-of-mouse" referrals) which lead to profitable new clients as well as valuable repeat business.

Building and promoting a brand identity – known in the trade as "branding" – is a technique all businesses and individuals can use to effectively market themselves and their services.

As a physician, your personal brand consists of how others perceive you and your practice, as well as the products and services you're offering. Branding is driven not only by how you provide services to your patients, but also how you communicate all of these elements to your target audiences.

At *beautiful forever,* we have successfully demonstrated with our clients that branding begins with your office – your physical plant, your staff, and your personal "bedside manner" in dealing with patients and prospects. However, branding goes far beyond what you actually deliver.

Branding includes your website and your social media web presence, your success in creating positive public and media relations (i.e., press coverage), and even your advertising. A decade ago, branding would have been influenced by your Yellow Pages ad as well, but thanks to the pervasiveness of the Internet (and especially your practice website) that is no longer a significant factor in branding.

Finally, your branding is driven by what your patients communicate to others. For example, although he'd innovated a new and now widespread laparoscopic procedure, one successful west coast bariatric surgeon's brand is defined more by the fact that one famous pop singer dedicated her well-received autobiography to him than by his reputation as a gifted innovator among fellow bariatric surgeons.

In the realm of branding, "perception is reality." Patients are seldom capable of determining for themselves the objective professional skill and quality of a given physician. Rather, they determine who is right for them based on their perception of that physician's personal and professional brand.

Regardless of how it is created, as a physician, your personal brand is very powerful because it sends a clear, consistent message about who you are and what you have to offer. A strong, authentic and compelling personal brand helps you become known for what you're good at.

It sets you apart from every other physician in your specialty, and a strong and positive brand can even position you as a niche expert, someone sought out by patients and prospects.

One of the quickest ways we have found at *beautiful forever* in working with our physician clients to jump-start the creation of your personal brand is to have the public identify you with that special factor by which you'd prefer to be known. What is that one thing by which you would like to be known?

Do you want to be known as caring and compassionate? Or would you rather be known as having a special area of expertise?

Do you want to be known as the best in your field in a certain procedure? Or would you rather be known as a gifted generalist who can "do it all?"

Your brand – how your target audiences perceive you – will either be one you consciously create, or one that is imposed upon you based on how you perform with your patients and how you market yourself. For most physicians, a consciously-created brand is far more powerful, and far more valuable, than one imposed on you by others.

So how do you go about creating a brand?

First, your brand must be based on measurable reality – it should be based on the kind of patient service that you constantly and faithfully deliver. However, your brand must also be something that is easily identifiable – a complex, carefully-nuanced "brand" will not be easily communicated or perceived. Instead, your brand should be clear, concise, and an accurate reflection of the physician you are.

Creating Your Brand

When it comes to creating your brand, you should begin by defining your personal and practice objective – who you are and what service you want to be known for.

Next, create your branding message. Begin, as Shakespeare said, with the idea that "to thine own self be true" – your branding message must be authentic. In addition, it must speak directly to your target market – it must be relevant to the people you wish to reach and to serve. Your brand is a promise of an outcome and a commitment to deliver on that commitment.

Patients respond when they can place their trust in your brand.

Having identified your desired brand, you should select the branding tools that will both communicate your message and reach your targets where they can be found. Does your prospective patients respond to word-of-mouth, or do they rely on the Internet for guidance? Do they respond to favorable press coverage or persuasive testimonials? Select the right blend of branding tools to convey your message.

This begins with your office – its location (are you on Park Avenue or Main Street?) – and with its design and décor. Your staff conveys your brand by the way they interact with patients and prospects, and you set the ultimate tone of your practice branding message. But beyond that, you need to make optimum use of your marketing and communications efforts.

Do you offer discounts to build volume, or do you present an exclusive and "it may cost more, but it's worth it" attitude of premium service at premium prices? All of these factors impact your brand.

Once you've defined your desired brand, you must consistently deliver on that brand's unique promise. Your brand messaging must be clear, consistent, and compelling. Inconsistent brand messaging destroys the most important aspect of a brand – delivering a value promise your patients can trust

Only by focusing on, and consistently delivering, your brand messaging will you be able to build a positive and lasting brand that earns trust from your target audiences.

Some steps *beautiful forever* has found that can be counted on to help deliver the brand you want to communicate include:

- Develop a great logo (including a color scheme and a look-and-feel for visual communications) – supported by consistent graphic standards – then display your logo and graphic standards prominently and consistently

- Put your key brand messages in writing, and make sure that every staff member delivers on your brand attributes

- Communicate your brand message in your website, in what your staff wears, how they answer the phone, your sales and advertising materials, promotions and special offers – every communications should reflect your brand

- Develop and use a tagline – a concise statement that captures the essence of your brand

- Deliver on your brand promise – make sure you're consistent in every interaction with your patients

First Impressions

Your website is your introduction to most prospects, so be consistent in the images that you use. Ensure that they reflect and reinforce your brand.

People will immediately get a feel for what you have to offer – you may have as little as 10 seconds to communicate that brand.

To assess your website's visceral brand message, view your site through the eyes of a new visitor. If it does not immediately "make the case" for your desired brand message, redesign that website so your message and identity are immediately unmistakable.

Then make sure your office (and your office staff) reflects your website – from your building exterior and geo-location to the design of your lobby, your office will either reinforce or shatter your developing brand image.

Social Media

Building your brand using social media allows you to develop new – and strengthen existing – relationships, leading to brand awareness, reinforced loyalty and word-of-mouth marketing.

Your Social Networking efforts will be designed to lead people to your website, which is your front-line branding too. Before you launch a Social Networking outreach effort, make sure your website reflects your brand.

Social Networking is made up of "content" and "conversation," and each is necessary to an effective campaign. Content tools include WordPress or Blogger blogs and YouTube video blogs, as well as white papers, case studies (i.e., testimonials) and even eBooks. Conversation includes posts on Facebook, Twitter and other discussion-oriented social networking sites, as well as posting comments on others' blogs.

Effective use of these tools will generate awareness, build interest and ultimately motivate a desired action – but improper use of these can prove disastrous. If you're not comfortable with Social Networking, find an expert who can help transform you from a gifted professional in the real world of medicine into an online "subject matter expert" or even a "thought leader," someone who others seek out for information on your areas of expertise.

Once you have your website in order and once you are creating memorable and valuable content, focus your conversation where it can be found by your target markets. Your success in Social Networking will depend on providing useful information and on developing relationships with members of your target audience.

Those who think of Social Networking as another useful self-promotion tool will be sadly disappointed – let others sing your praises, but refrain from blowing your own horn.

Rebranding

At *beautiful forever*, one of our most important roles in helping our clients involves rebranding. While some brands are carefully planned, many physician practices have brands that "just happened," without any conscious planning. The doctor provides services that reflect his or her style, the staff does the best they can (based on their personal skills), but without a lot of direction or leadership.

Too often, the brand reflected by a practice's office location and décor "just happened," too. Frequently, it seems that the website, the brochures, the ways practices communicate with their clients are based on "I've got a brother-in-law who can do your website," plus what the product reps provide to pass out. Success is a matter of luck, more than planning.

When such a client retains us, we advise them to start at the beginning, and to re-invent themselves (with our help and guidance) to become the doctor – and the practice – they always wanted to be. The steps we at *beautiful forever* have identified as the best way to succeed in re-branding include:

- Identify, very specifically, the brand you want to project for yourself and your practice – then take steps to start presenting that brand image to patients and prospects.

- Look at your location – the address, the physical dimensions, and most important, the look-and-feel – of your office. Everything that stands in the way of presenting the right brand must be eliminated, or fixed. If you're locked into a long-term lease, this means providing an office "face-lift" and "make-over," just as you'd provide to a patient, so that it looks the best it can, based on what you have to work with.

- Retrain the staff (and this can mean re-shuffling the staff, or even replacing people who just cannot fit with the "brand") so that every staff member, in dealing with every patient or prospect, reflects the brand image you want to project.

- Start over with your website – replace somebody's brother-in-law with a real professional who can make it reflect your brand, accurately and consistently. Then go a step further and retain an SEO professional to help position that website so prospects will find it, and retain a marketing and promotion professional (this is a service *beautiful forever* offers, so our clients don't need to take this step) to get your website and your practice the attention you need to succeed.

- Start over with your patient hand-outs – brochures, forms, etc. – and with any proprietary products you sell in your office, so that all of them reflect your brand as well. Only use product brochures provided by reps if they reflect your brand – if they do not, create your own. Consistency is vital.

- Finally, work with past and current patients to encourage them to refer you new prospects – confident that your new brand image will not only generate new business, but that when your former patients understand who you really are (remember, your brand reflects reality), they'll come back for more services.

Conclusion

If you first identify the brand you want, then create actions and images which reflect that brand, you will succeed in branding yourself and your practice, and will find this leads to more "qualified" prospects – potential patients who actually want what you have to offer.

It is a process – it takes time and consistency – but done properly, it is the most reliable and effective marketing and practice-building tool in your arsenal.

Section Six: Networking

Successful Aesthetics Medical Practice Networking

This chapter is based on a series of presentations and articles I have given before professional conferences in 2012 and 2013.

Introduction – What is Networking?

Networking is one of the more effective Medical Practice or business marketing tools, because it is in-your-face personal, and because it creates human bonds that will lead to trust – and more business.

By definition, "networking" involves developing contacts and exchanging information with other people. Unlike social interactions intended to develop personal friendships, networking is done for purposes of developing business.

To be successful, your networking must be genuine and authentic. It must build trust. At its core, networking builds a reciprocal relationship – it is all about how you can help others, as well about as how others can help you.

To be successful, before you go to a networking event or even meet someone casually, you should also have a goal in mind, results-oriented, and it should be presented with enthusiasm.

Why should you spend your time networking?

There are a number of excellent reasons for networking, but they all add up to building your business, thereby generating additional profitable revenue.

Some of the specific reasons include:

- Growing your marketing database

- Becoming known by "those who count" in target niche markets

- Increasing the number of referrals prospective patients

- Building profitable relationships

- Increasing product and service sales

- Enhancing your brand

- Building your reputation, leading to favorable word-of-mouth

Traditionally, networking has involved meeting people face to face at chamber of commerce meetings, civic clubs and other social/business events.

Technology has expanded your networking opportunities – today, you can effectively network via LinkedIn, Facebook, Twitter, Google Plus and other social networking sites.

Social networking is no longer merely helpful. It has become essential to aesthetic business and Medical Practice success. However, nothing can replace the impact of positive human interactions.

Face to face meetings rapport and connect individuals in ways that social networking cannot.

Mastering Networking – Where do I Begin?

Because of its importance in Medical Practice building, mastering the networking process is a low-cost and high-impact way of growing your aesthetics business. Create what is known in the trade as an "elevator pitch" – a brief introduction to you and to your Medical Practice or aesthetics business.

In less than 30 seconds, your elevator pitch must make your listener want to learn more about you. Find ways to differentiate yourself from others in your field. Give specifics about what you do. If you have are in a niche market with special skills and talents, mention that.

Be memorable.

Because your elevator pitch is your door-opener, practice it on staff, family members or friends, and keep working on it until you're comfortable with it.

Physician-to-physician referrals remain among the strongest and most effective referrals. Focus first on nurturing your relationship with professionals who currently refer to you, then expand your network by meeting and attracting other professionals into your referral network.

When networking, start with phone calls and professional-to-professional handwritten notes, followed up with emails. Build toward asking for relationship-building face-to-face meetings in times and places convenient for the other professional.

Once you've established your professional referral network, become comfortable asking network members to introduce you to prospects. Done right, asking for these introductions will not be seen as being pushy, over-aggressive or inappropriate. As with the "elevator pitch," practice asking for referrals on staff, family members or friends, and keep practicing until you're comfortable with the process.

This same approach can be followed as you include others into your network of potential referral sources. These should include non-medical health-related professionals (chiropractors, podiatrists, etc.), aesthetics-related business owners, salon and spa owners and others who are in a position to make qualified referrals.

The best places to network are professional society events where you'll meet individuals just like you, people who work in your field and share common interests and knowledge. These are great places to meet potential collaborators.

However there are other places that also work in reaching out to prospects and referral sources, including:

- Corporate health fair

- Charity wine tastings

- Hospital or healthcare fund-raising events

- Gallery openings

- Classical music concerts

Networking Groups

When you are ready to reach out beyond your professional society to network with other potential members of your network, start locally. Patients will come from a geographic area – generally within five to 10 miles of your office.

Many civic and business groups offer an online member listing with profiles; review this list to see if the organization is a good fit before investing time and resources. Civic, cultural and business groups often meet once a month – generally around a meal – while others hold mixers. Groups will often allow you to attend meetings or events as a guest, at least at first.

In selecting networking groups, ask yourself a few questions about the group's ability to help you network successfully, such as:

- Does this group put you in contact with strategic partners?

- Does it attract your potential customer?

- Does it offer training in new skills that will help you find new business?

Only focus on groups that fulfill the screening criteria you selected. Then, when you're ready to start networking, visit as many of those groups as possible, and look for other criteria, such as:

- Does the group have a comfortable (to you) tone and attitude?

- Do you feel welcome – could you see yourself actually being productive in this group meeting?

- Are the members seem supportive of one another?

- Does the group seem to have competent leadership?

When evaluating formal networking groups, visit appropriate groups few times before joining. Arrive at the meeting early and stay late. While there, participate – that's what networking is all about.

Even though you're there to help grow your business, don't come across as someone who is only self-involved. Become known as a helpful and respected resource. Once you commit to the group, if possible, consider hosting a meeting – having prospects or referral sources in your office can be a big plus.

Also consider if you might be able to provide a program yourself, or sponsor a speaker. Should people give you referrals, follow through quickly and efficiently, and do so with the utmost respect and professionalism, and keep your referral source in the loop.

Remember that your actions are a reflection on your referral source.

When and How to Network

PTAs and School Functions – and Kids Sports Leagues – These bring out the proverbial soccer moms, women with an active lifestyle who may want help looking their best. Networking here "hits them where they live."

Corporate Health Fairs – these are excellent places to meet employed women with income and resources – and a sense of competition for the next promotion that might encourage a more youthful appearance. This can apply to both men and women, and this makes these fairs an excellent place to network.

Leisure Time – Networking during leisure activities works well for professionals – office hours have other priorities. Golf, tennis and other activities can create a potential bond that leads to referrals.

Volunteering – Pick a rewarding cause then take a leadership position that will help you stay visible. It's an example of doing well by doing good.

Alumni Events – There is a not-unreasonable expectation that alumni will help one another. So, if your alumni association meets locally, you have a ready-made connection.

Women Only Groups – Some women's networking groups are long-established, while others are fairly new; some are online only, while others hold in-person events or offer one-on-one mentoring.

Airport/Airplane – Don't underestimate the value of using this "down time" in a plane or at a gate effectively.

Civic organization – Civic organizations with a purpose you can support are great places to build relationships with others, and to help the community at the same time.

Internet Business Networking Websites – In the 21st Century, this may be the most obvious networking tool of all. Social networking sites are open 24/7, and they make it fairly easy to locate people with similar interests. Online ties can be weaker than in-person relationships, but they are a place to start.

Blogging – Your goal by networking online is to become seen by target audiences as a "subject matter expert" or "thought leader" – someone who people turn to with confidence in areas of your expertise.

This requires a two-phased program – creating and posting "content" (blogs, video blogs, case studies, white papers, white-board videos, webinars, eBooks, etc.) and then using the social media to generate "conversation" that promotes the content while positioning you as an expert. Most professionals find that the time involved makes professional "ghost writers" to create the "content" – and the "conversation" that promotes it effectively to your target audiences.

Social media sites useful in promoting aesthetics Medical Practices and businesses include:

LinkedIn – Whatever your business objectives, LinkedIn will help you to build a network of useful contacts. People are on LinkedIn with the sole purpose of connecting for business reasons. LinkedIn's subject-matter groups represent an effective way to position yourself as a subject matter expert, and to invite people to view your blogs and other content.

Facebook and Twitter – These interactive conversational sites are more places to connect with consumers – patients and prospects – than with professional referral sources.

Pinterest and Instagram – These are relatively new and fast-growing social media sites that are more visually-oriented, and therefore better for posting before-and-after case study material.

Create and Nurture Network Relationships

People are not truly part of your network until you have created a perceived relationship with them. Within 24 hours of meeting someone in person, follow up with them via phone, email, text or some other means of communications. Then continue to nurture this new relationship with information (emails, text), invitations (have them join you on social media sites) and in other ways to help grow that relationship. This is where the conversational side of social media can prove helpful.

Making it Personal – Set Up a Meeting

If a prospective network member seems likely to be able to provide valuable referrals, make that relationship personal by scheduling a follow-up meeting. Pick a neutral meeting location (i.e., not your office, or theirs) that is convenient for the other party – a restaurant or coffee shop usually works. Don't be late, and be sure to pay the bill – after all, you're the host.

These initial meetings should not be just about work, nor should they be just about you. Focus on interpersonal subjects that will help to build this new relationship, and talk about things that you both find interesting. Be sure to pay close attention to their body language. If that the other person seems to be losing interest, change the topic.

This first meeting – as well as follow up meetings – is one of the keys to successful networking. If this person is worth courting for your referral network, you'll have to plan on more meetings. Networking relationships take time to build.

Conclusion – Networking Pays Off

With time and effort, networking will materially grow your business. Plan on growing your business by developing a workable blend of social networking and face-to-face networking. Consider the rewards of a solid new referral source, and be prepared to put in the time and resources necessary to nurture that referral source as a member of your network.

Section Six: Mystery Shopping

Mystery Shopping

The Best Way to See Yourself as Others See You ... And to Assess Your Brand

The Scottish poet Robert Burns wrote about the wonderful gift of "seeing yourself as others see you." For a doctor's Medical Practice, it is often difficult to accurately and objectively know how your prospects and patients actually see you.

Yet that information is vital for the success of your business and professional Medical Practice.

One of the most effective ways of determining how patients and prospects see you is through the eyes of a professional "mystery shopper."

The basic "mystery shop" involves having a trained professional mystery shopper call the Medical Practice, posing as a prospect, then ask questions and make an appointment. A more in-depth and useful "mystery shop" involves having that same trained professional mystery shopper actually come in and experience a preliminary assessment.

 Either way, that professional then completes a detailed Mystery Shopping Checklist, and follows that up with a detailed report.

The key to a successful "mystery shop" is to use trained and professional mystery shoppers who really understand the process as it applies to a Medical Practice.

Professional mystery shoppers have experience in helping physicians "mystery shop" their Medical Practices – helping them to identify their brand – as their brand is seen by their prospects and patients. Then, if image problems exist, they help the physicians to re-brand their Medical Practices.

The goal is to make sure that the physicians' perceived brand image is in synch with the image they'd like to present to patients and prospects.

To facilitate this process, I have developed and included in the Appendix a Mystery Shopping Checklist which, when completed by a professional mystery shopper, will help you determine if your brand reflects the image you'd like to present.

Section Seven: Human Resources

Top 5 Strategies for HR Success

There is a reason they call it *Human Resources*

This chapter was based on a presentation created for Med-Spa owners to help them improve both internal operations and external sales.

You've been successfully running a Medical Practice, so expanding to include a medical spa should be easy considering you already have a great staff in place, right? Not exactly. The secret behind every successful medical spa practice is "culture-specific" planning.

Take the time to plan for the unique culture of a medical spa by creating a strategic framework within which you will work. Focus on both the retail nature of the medical spa business and the people you will choose to help you run your Medical Practice.

With a clear understanding of the aesthetic culture and a commitment to human resource management, your move to expand into the exciting medical spa industry should be a smooth one.

You are holding the key to medical spa success

Use Key Performance Indicators to unlock your business potential

You have a brilliant mission statement and a stellar Medical Practice vision, as well as superbly defined organizational goals. But how will you measure your progress? Tie your goals to key performance indicators (KPIs) and just watch where they can take you – and your business.

Collecting, analyzing and making use of key performance indicators is what keeps a business moving in the right direction.

By locking key performance indicators into every goal in your business plan, then following through by measuring the outcomes, you can adjust or get rid of what isn't working and identify exactly where to put your efforts for even greater success.

It's About Time

Managing Time to Increase Medical Spa Productivity

We all start with the same 24 hours, but it is how we manage those hours that set the stage for our success. The rewards of developing a time management program within your Medical Practice include higher productivity and the fulfillment of the goals and objectives you set forth in your business plan.

On a day-to-day basis, time management helps prioritize everyday tasks, eliminate unnecessary activities and manage personal as well as professional time more efficiently.

Project Management
Your Key to Success – No Matter How the Economy Drives Demand

In the "good ole' days," bottom line meant bottom line. That is, when you asked, "How are we doing?" a simple answer involved looking at the financial outcome. Well, these are certainly not the "good ole' days," and you need to know how your Medical Practice is performing and how far it can go.

In today's economic environment, sound project management is no longer just a competitive advantage; it is an essential tool for survival.

With project management protocols in place, you have the keys to meet your Medical Practice goals on time and on budget.

And that gives you more time to concentrate on keeping your patients happy – and coming back for more.

Policies and Procedures
The "Why" and "How" of Success That Will Keep Your Medical Practice on Track

You have firmly established – and internalized – the purpose of your aesthetic Medical Practice; now, you need to develop a clear and measurable set of policies and procedures with which to run it. Not only does your Medical Practice require a written guide, but also the training and incentives to keep your staff on board and ensure your procedures are used.

Further, continuous testing and measuring of your progress is vital so you can take your Medical Practice beyond maintenance (acceptable success) and move to the next level.

Section Eight: Staff Sales Programs

The Aesthetic Consultation
Setting the Stage for Beautiful Results

This chapter was developed for a series of published articles on sales in the Medical Practice.

"You are the best and I will recommend you to everyone!"

These are exactly the words you want to hear from every patient, so it is vital that you put the time and effort into making sure the patient experience is beyond compare from beginning to end. Fine-tuning your consultation process is one way to help ensure your success – and each patient's happiness with the results.

Every consultation should follow a step-by-step protocol to determine what the patient wants and needs so you and your staff can design an appropriate treatment plan. Every member of your staff should be trained to follow the same procedure for every consultation.

This includes assessing potential issues that might preclude a particular procedure, as well as providing suggestions for additional procedures and products that can enhance the final results. Most importantly, the consultation allows you to set expectations with the patient – an important step that can help increase a patient's level of satisfaction with the outcome.

What is your motivation?

Remember that customer service is essential in a business with lots of competitors, so it is important to get into the right mindset before the consultation even begins. First, remove the word "sell" from your vocabulary and remember that the consult is all about the patient and what he or she desires. Review these important points before each and every consultation:

- This is a conversation to explore if and/or how your Medical Practice can be of assistance to this patient.

- Your Medical Practice is most concerned about what services and products will best serve this patient.

- You are willing to put yourself in this patient's skin so you can see things from his or her perspective.

- The consultation room is a place where you really listen.

- This is all about the patient.

- Consultation is a process you enjoy and feel good about.

By approaching each consultation with these things in mind, you and your staff will come across as authentic, caring and committed.

Exactly the type of place your patients want to go for treatments, services and products.

Staging the consultation room

The consultation is your practice's opportunity to really shine. Not only will you be able to offer your services and products, but also show that yours is a nurturing and professional environment in which the patient can place the utmost trust.

That means the setting must fit the bill.

Create a comfortable and non-threatening consult room where you can build rapport in a relaxed manner. Once you have greeted the patient (in a timely fashion that is respectful of his or her time), offer a refreshing and healthful beverage. Do not rush the consult.

In fact, you may want to make it a standard practice to book a full hour for consultations even when you may only need 30 minutes.

Don't forget to make use of technology to enhance the process, such as a PowerPoint presentation of a procedure or a slide show of before-and-after photos of your patients.

Also, special pricing for seasonal offers, such as sclerotherapy to get ready for summer, should be prominently displayed.

The script
Not just a series of questions and answers

"Address your first question to yourself: if you could press a magic button and get every piece of information you want, what would you want to know? The answer will immediately help you compose the right questions," says Russell Webster in *Super Communication: The NLP Way.*

Approaching every consultation this way will be the key to unlocking the patient's needs, desires and objections. But remember, a successful consultation is not just about asking questions, it is about building a relationship and knowing what to ask and when.

A technique called engaged inquiry is a great way of gaining rapport with your patients. The key is to set aside judgments, assumptions and reactions as they arise and ask questions so that you are able to gain the information necessary to fully understand what the patient is telling you.

Your goal? To help you determine the actual needs of each individual in an interactive way.

Engaged inquiry is designed to help you find the right service or product fit for each individual patient. Once you uncover his or her wants, needs and values, you will be better prepared to present the best options available. In addition to gathering information, engaged inquiry also helps:

- Build trust and rapport

- Keep the patient focused

- Ensure that the patient feels like part of the solution

- Allow the consultant to personalize the services and products that will best meet the unique needs, wants and values of the patient

Never assume a thing that you can learn by asking. Ask open-ended questions rather than the "yes or no" variety. Ask for clarification, "Could you be more specific about that?"

Because this also is the time and place for the patient to ask questions, it is absolutely essential to know everything there is to know about the services and products your Medical Practice provides. If you are counting on your staff to perform consultations, they should be able to show each patient how the service or product will benefit him or her.

When consultants know your services and products inside and out, not only can they explain how they work, but also handle any questions or objections a patient may have.

In leading the patient to make a good decision regarding aesthetic services, education is the key. Use the consultation to teach the patient about the options available and their expected benefits, along with the time and any discomfort involved, including potential side effects.

Pre- and post-procedure skin care regimen should also be carefully discussed. This provides an opportunity for post-treatment repeat office visits to purchase skin care products, as well as future aesthetic services.

Quiet on the set!

You know what to ask, so really take the time to listen for the answers. It can be tough to do for many of us because we can hear 450-600 words per minute, while the person we are listening to is only speaking about 125 words per minute.

That means we have all kinds of time to start formulating a response and we may actually stop listening. Instead of thinking about what you will be saying next, use the time you are silent to really listen.

(The words "silent" and "listen" share the same letters. Keep them firmly in mind during each consultation).

"I find that empathetic listening helps me to understand the patient's thought process as well as their needs; and this helps me give them good advice which usually leads to a sale," says Marcy Street MD, Medical Director of Doctor's Approach Dermatology and Laser Center and creator of Doctor's Approach Skin and Hair Care in Michigan.

- Become a better listener and stay more focused on what your patient is saying with the following tips:

- Be careful about interrupting when your patient is speaking – generally, it is better to hear them out before refocusing them.

- Maintain eye contact.

- Clarify what the patient has said by asking follow-up questions or rephrasing what he or she has said.

- Listen for solutions.

- Explore the meaning behind conflicting statements.

- Listen for:

  o What is missing.

  o Concerns the patient may have or what is important to them.

  o What he or she values.

  o What he or she wants and needs in order to fill in the gap between what he or she has now and what is desired.

(Adapted from Keith Rosen, Executive Sales Coach, Profit Builders)

You are certain to encounter objections, so employ the Feel-Felt-Found technique. With it, you can recognize the objection, sympathize with it and then share a simple solution.

For example, if a patient has answered questions in a way that shows she wants the benefits of a particular service, but is concerned about the cost, you could respond with, "I understand how you feel.

In fact, many of our patients felt the same way at first, but they found the results from this procedure were long lasting and actually more cost effective than other options."

Engaged inquiry requires asking and listening, both of which may require additional training for you and/or your staff. Some simple role-playing can help you and your staff better develop – and even master – these skills.

To book or not to book?

Be aware of any telltale signs that a patient is ready to make a final decision and book an appointment – even if you feel you have more to say on the subject. Avoid offering more reasons for a patient to say yes – you then run the risk of either confusing the patient or causing him or her to lose interest and tune you out.

There are some generally accepted booking signals that you can look for, including when a patient:

- Spends time looking at one service or product over others that have been offered

- Asks questions about the details

- Asks about price and/or financing

- Uses possession language

- Asks about other patients' experiences or opinions

- Takes out a date book or wallet

There are also signals that tell you that a patient is not ready to move forward, including:

- Avoiding eye contact with you

- Making 'not now' excuses

- Casually handling the product or collateral material

- Looking at many different services or products

When a patient is not ready to make a final decision at the end of your consultation, carefully (and quickly) review what may have gone wrong, then take steps to correct it. Have you listened closely enough to what the patient hopes to achieve? Have you offered the right service or product? You may still have time to meet the patient's needs by reviewing what you have already talked about.

Ask him or her, to tell you again what it is that he or she is hoping to achieve so you can find the right fit. Then listen.

People do have different decision making styles and you are sure to see them all. Some purchase based solely on logic. Others wish to fill an emotional need. And still others base their decision on how their choice will look to others. Listen and watch for the cues so you can further individualize your consultation.

The Final Act

Some patients will tell you they want to set the appointment or purchase the product before you can formulate the question. Everyone else will need to be asked. Remember to maintain eye contact, and be polite, sincere and respectful.

For example, you may say, "So, Sue, from what we have discussed, you are most interested in the dermal filler. When would you like to schedule time for these procedures? Is next Tuesday or Wednesday better for you?" If an appointment must be set in another part of the office, you should either call in the staff member who handles the appointments or walk the patient to him or her.

But remember – we can't stress this too much – everyone wants to buy, but nobody wants to feel like they are being sold.

With every patient, remember that every prospect can review you online – quality interpersonal presentations are important. This touches on reputation management, an entirely different issue, but an important one. Do your best to make sure, whether you sell them or not, that they are satisfied – happy – with the experience.

If you have properly educated the patient and addressed their needs and concerns, they will naturally be ready to set the date. If they will purchase a series of treatments, this is the time to obtain a commitment for the whole series in order to give the "package" price.

For those who say they want to think about it, be sure to send a personalized follow-up note. Include specifics from the consultation to ensure that the patient knows you remember them, their goals and objectives. Then set up a follow-up phone call.

The patient should know you will be calling so they will not feel harassed. Find out the best time and day for the call and be sure to send the patient a marketing package specific to the patient's needs. The follow up call should be made by the same patient-coordinator who did the consult.

Finally, don't forget why the patient has come to your Medical Practice in the first place. If you can provide the finest services and products along with a generous and caring manner, you will continue to build a successful Medical Practice one consultation after another.

Turning Your Employees into Sales Agents

You know the value of good word-of-mouth, so you work hard to make sure your patients are treated right. But, even with all that effort, unless your employees are all motivated "sales agents," your Medical Practice is still missing out on valuable selling opportunities.

This can translate into thousands of dollars in lost revenue every month. If your patients are happy with the services you provide – if they trust you (and they do) – they actually want to be sold on your other services. That actually adds to their overall satisfaction.

Providing your staff with the proper training to transform them into customer-centered sales agents is one of the best investments in your practice's growth that you can make.

To maximize your profits – while maximizing patient satisfaction – it is imperative that your staff members know how to promote your Medical Practice. They need to know about your full range of services, and they need to know how to book current and prospective patients for at least a consultation, and do that on the spot.

This equates to blending customer service with sales – and it is that blending that makes all the difference.

This seminar focuses on ways you can train your staff to sell, up-sell, cross-sell – and to convert more leads into consultations. We will show you what your staff needs to be doing EVERY time they interact with a patient or prospect.

Develop Your Customer Service Skills

Customer Service is the sum total of what an organization does to meet your customers' expectations, and to produce customer satisfaction.

That is the feeling your customers gets when they are happy with the service they have been provided. Customer Satisfaction can be a strong differentiator between you and your competition.

Recognize the benefits to your Medical Practice which include:

- Staff loyalty

- Patient loyalty

- Patient referral

How is this accomplished? Learn how by choosing the right people to work for you, communication and leading from the top.

Business you're not getting
The best external marketing starts internally

Even the most successful physician Medical Practices often concentrate too much on external marketing. As a result, physicians often lose focus of their most powerful marketing opportunity – their patient's total office experience.

Internal marketing – which includes staff-to-patient selling – is a strong Medical Practice enhancement tool. It can deliver an even more powerful punch than external marketing in your pursuit for loyal patients. Its cost-to-benefit ratio is one that simply cannot be beat.

Learn how to impact the success of your Medical Practice and watch your patient base grow!

Motivation – the Key to Sales Success

There is an old adage in sales: Sales Performance is made up of equal portions of Sales Ability and Sales Motivation. And the oft-overlooked truth is this: The most skillful sales person on earth won't close many deals if she's not properly motivated, if the incentivization for success isn't there.

If your Medical Practice is interested in increasing sales and productivity, then a staff incentive program will help you achieve this goal. To achieve sales growth, you must ensure that your salespeople are properly motivated – and sales incentives are a great motivator. They should also remember that everybody wants to buy, but nobody wants to be sold.

This is no secret. Department stores that sell cosmetics and beauty aids learned several generations ago that sales reps and product demonstrators who were properly incentivized – with their incentive (usually a sales commission) tied to sales performance – achieved far higher sales success than is achieved with salaried or hourly sales people.

Macy's, Gimbels, Saks, Nordstrom's and other traditionally successful stores which offered premium cosmetics and beauty aids all motivate their sales staffs with commissions, bonuses and other direct-reward means of recognizing superior sales success.

In medical practices and spas, compensation packages have to recognize that several staff members may have helped in the sale – including the physician – and, as a result, customized sliding-scale compensation packages should be developed for your specific needs. This is best done by an outside expert who has handled this many times before.

Spas and physician Medical Practices that offer branded or up-scale commercial cosmetics and beauty aids typically achieve much more impressive sales success when their sales reps are financially-motivated by sales. The same is often true for staff members who are responsible for selling – or up-selling – services such as Botox and other injectables, or laser treatments.

In fact, any service that is sold based on the patient's personal desire (as opposed to those based on medical necessity) are more successfully sold when staff members responsible for sales are incentivized and rewarded for closing deals.

In developing compensation plans, it is important that the plans be clear and straightforward, and that they be fair to all concerned. While it is possible to create healthy competition among staff members, too much focus on competition among staff members for commissions, bonuses and other compensation can prove counterproductive in terms of staff morale and overall performance. While sales is an important metric, it is not the only important factor in staff performance. Service quality must also be rewarded.

However, properly structured, competition for staff success and advancement that's based on an incentive plan can create an environment where everyone works harder and strives to do their best. If staff members understand their incentive plan – and if they recognize that their performance is being measured for purposes of compensation and advancement – then the benefits far outweigh the risks or problems such competition may create.

Incentive programs which tie employee performance to employee rewards – whether that performance is measured in terms of sales or in client service – can produce a win-win system for spas and cosmetic/aesthetic Medical Practices. As a means of recognition, a carefully thought-out and fairly implemented incentive plan increases employee productivity, loyalty, and morale.

By combining performance and reward, your Medical Practice attracts and retains motivated and entrepreneurial employees who are goal-driven. This can create a Medical Practice that is far more productive – and a far happier place to work – than one where employee rewards are tied to those who just show up to get a paycheck.

As has been demonstrated by both Nordstrom's-like organizations and profitable aesthetics Medical Practices and medical spas, well-established methods of paying commissions – and, in the process – holding employees accountable for their performance can work very effectively in motivating performance and profitability in a medical aesthetic business.

A key element to this success depends on the quality of the training that is provided to employees, both when they join the Medical Practice and on an ongoing basis. For instance, employees who are being incentivized or bonus-rewarded for sales success will require ongoing sales training in order to achieve their personal performance and financial goals.

Equally, employees who are being incentivized for the successful provision of patient care services need to be trained – and re-trained – on what it means to effectively deliver those services. "Performance" should never be a given, nor should the ability to perform be assumed of all new employees.

However, while many times employees perform better with incentives, it is important to remember that money doesn't always have to be the primary objective. There are several ways for employees to know that the harder and more effectively they work the more they can earn.

- Cash bonus: Not surprising, money is the best reward for most salespeople.

- Merchandise: Sometimes people are more excited by the hot item of the moment, than by the equivalent amount of money. This can also apply to services provided by the Medical Practice. Some employees will want aesthetic services to enhance their own appearance, and will work harder in hopes of being rewarded with injectables, laser treatments or other services.

- Experience: Offering an experience – such as an all-expense paid vacation, a plane trip, or hot sports or rock-concert tickets – can create memories that last forever.

- Recognition: Taking the time to recognize a leading performer with an award or a special luncheon or party. In terms of expense, for those Medical Practices on a limited budget, this will cost less than commission incentives. However, if everyone is recognized, the incentive factor will be minimized – but if some are left out, that too can create morale problems. Rewards are most effective when tied to direct and measurable actions.

- Workplace privileges: Give your top performers their own room, paid education or any kind of workplace flexibility that they would value.

When it comes to any kind of ongoing incentive program, it is important to make keep the incentives simple – and the performance that are tied to those incentives should be easy to understand and track. Complex programs – as well as programs that lack fairness or invite favoritism – can de-motivate employees.

To be effective in motivating desired performance, incentives must be clear, fairly administrated and directly tied to measurable performance. Especially when it comes to commissions, how they are earned – and paid out – must be as straightforward as possible. Nothing destroys morale more quickly than an employee thinking she's earned a commission payment that she doesn't receive.

The first step in developing a workable and effective incentive program involves defining the minimum gross profit your Medical Practice must produce in order to maintain its return on your investment – and that investment includes capital investments and the time you put into creating and sustaining the Medical Practice. When considering employee compensation, the amount of the incentive should be calculated based on the gross profit generated by the incentivized performance.

For instance:

- If a service costs $100 per procedure in terms of hard costs, including overhead costs; and,

- If that service costs $100 in terms of staff compensation (physician and employee); and,

- If the service generates compensation of $500; then,

- A commission of 10% to 20% ($50 to $100) is not unrealistic – it will leave you with a gross profit of $200 to $250, or 40% to 50%. However, a commission of 40% would generate a gross profit of 20%, and would reflect a relatively poor return on investment.

Again, a customized, practice-specific or spa-specific compensation plan is probably the better way to go. It will help build sales, strengthen loyalty and improve morale.

The way to hold employees accountable is to have a program that rewards good performance and negatively impacts the incentive amount if the performance is below expectations. For example, if an employee maintains production numbers higher than what is established by management, the incentive paid to the employee increases. If the numbers fall short, the incentive is decreased.

Your customized incentive plan should reward all employees of the Medical Practice based on their specific contributions to the overall success – the greater the responsibilities/ or productivity, the greater the reward. This incentive/reward program includes senior positions, clinical employees, aesthetician and administrative personnel.

While sales commission may be the basis for the plan, not all employees will be closing sales – but if they are part of the service delivery program, they should also be incentivized.

An example from outside the sales commission world can be found in restaurants where tips – paid to the wait-staff, who have the primary client contact role – are shared with all staff responsible for providing a premium guest experience. In this way, cooks and busboys, as well as waitresses, are rewarded for an overall positive patron experience.

This same concept should be included in the overall Medical Practice incentive program. The nurse or tech who provides quality services should be in line for compensation in the same way that the sales clerk who sold the patient on the service should be compensated.

To avoid morale problems or conflicts, rewards should be provided on a consistent basis. This could be on a per-unit basis, or on a time – monthly or quarterly – basis. Consistency and reliability helps to maintain motivation – it also reduces the administrative burden on management.

Many have found that keeping incentives flexible allows the rewards to evolve as your business grows. Rigid rewards can become obsolete or even counterproductive over time. However, changes should be positive and not punitive.

Another primary value of incentive plans can include the retention of your most desirable employees by rewarding them for helping the company succeed over time.

If you want your Medical Practice to grow, consider the role of commissions, bonuses or other financial incentives can plan as part of the overall package you are offering. Some of the more common packages are

- Commission only

- Commission plus salary

- Commission plus bonus or

- Commission plus salary plus bonus.

Keep in mind that in order to be effective, incentives must be tied to areas that employees have control over, and they must also be tied to those activities which promote the profitability of the Medical Practice.

Three Quick Tips to a More Successful Business

If you want to be successful, three simple tips for turning the business you have into the business you'd like to have will help jump-start you on the path to success – as simple as One-Two-Three ...

One – Ask For Referrals

There is no marketing tool more powerful than a referral from a satisfied client. Many people who would consider making referrals never even consider it – but if you ask them to tell their friends, or write a testimonial, or even record a brief video, they will gladly help you out.

Two: Reward Referrals

Referrals that turn into business will make you money – it's not unreasonable to "share the wealth" with those who bring you business. Offer discounts on future services, or even free products or services. Give them a reason to spread the word, and those who like you will build your business for you.

Three: Find Ways of Selling Clients Something New

The hardest buying decision is the first one. After clients have chosen you once, it is much easier for them to choose you again. Offer them incentives to buy, and buy again.

Chapter Two: Specializing a Business

While offering a general aesthetic Medical Practice can be an effective way of achieving success, in practical terms, most physicians and surgeons either specialize in a few types of procedures, or specialize in a single or a few related areas of the body. Others specialize in working with ethnic skin, or prefer injectables to surgery.

A key factor here is personal satisfaction – even a generalist will usually prefer performing some procedures more than others.

This all makes a case for specialization – and my team and I have seen many successful examples of specialization, even extreme specialization. Some doctors specialize in hands, or noses, eyes or breasts, love-handles or neck-wattles. Each specialization has supporters, and profitable ones at that.

In the next few chapters, I'll highlight some useful tips relating to specialization.

Section One: Ethnic and Niche Markets

Effectively Reaching Out to Ethnic and Niche Markets

It's Not Just Skin Color ...
Culture and "Orientation" Play Their Parts

One of the most significant challenge faced by any specialty aesthetics Medical Practice, spa or other business – especially during an extended economic downturn, such as we've been experiencing since 2007 – involves bringing in enough paying customers to keep the doors open, the lights on and the staff paid.

A distinctive answer to this challenge involves reaching out to specialty niche markets – these can be ethnic markets or other niche markets – but what makes them distinctive are a few factors:

- They have their own media, which reach them, but few others

- As minorities outside the mainstream, they tend to cluster together, making them easier to reach, and much easier to "ignite" word-of-mouth

- They tend to extend loyalty to those who reach out to them with respect and cultural sensitivity

In the aesthetics market, there are (typically) two kinds of niche markets. One of them is based on race, as reflected in skin tone and distinctive facial features. The other has to do with lifestyle choices and orientation.

As the Wall Street Journal reported on July 8, 2012, many retailers are reaching out to the latter group – specifically, Gays (to both Gay men and Gay women – which are very different markets) because this group has higher-than-average buying power, and because they understand the loyalty and word-of-mouth factors. Once Gays feel comfortable, respected

– even courted – at a retailer, they become brand-loyal and they tell their friends.

The WSJ also notes that there is a risk of backlash, from those not part of the group, and this can hurt business. For instance, while it is thankfully eroding away from our society's belief system, there is still a hostile attitude among some toward Gays, and if a business is seen too openly courting Gays, it might drive away those bigots.

However, there is a rejection beyond bigotry, and it applies to all ethnic and lifestyle- choice marketing efforts. That is the "do I belong here" issue. When you market to Gays, or to any ethnic minority, you are telling them, "you belong here – you are welcome here."

That is a very good thing. However, for every member of an ethnic minority who receives that message, those not of that minority hear a very different message – "This isn't for me, I don't belong here, I'm not welcome here."

This highlights both strengths and the weaknesses of marketing to various ethnic markets. Yet, there is a huge opportunity in the aesthetics world for expanding into the "ethnic skin color" and the "lifestyle-choice" markets, so it is worth considering in detail.

There are both risks and very real opportunities when it comes to marketing to ethnic and other specialty niche markets.

Here are some suggestions for successful marketing into those ethnic and specialty markets, tips which can be used effectively in attracting members of the target groups while minimizing the risk of alienating culturally-sensitive members of the mainstream market.

- Understand – really understand – what makes up that market

- Use the specialized ethnic media; do not go after narrow-cast target niche markets with broadcast marketing messages

- Use messages that are culturally-sensitized – ask members of that market to review the messages for unseen landmines

- Be ready to respond to prospects in a culturally-sensitive fashion – or adjust accordingly

- Create distinctive web page and collateral material intended just for members of the targeted ethnic group

Now, let's go through this list point by point:

Really understand the ethnic market. From the outside, all ethnic groups appear to be monolithic, but they are not. For instance, if you wanted to market to Cubans, as we do for our clients in South Florida, you'd need to realize that Cubans are not Mexicans – instead, they are very "European" in both heritage and mind-set. They have a racial mix that ranges from Nordic to Mediterranean Caribbean Indian to African-American – but they share a common culture which permits you to reach them without addressing ethnic distinctions.

But you'll only know this if you really understand the culture. We have also discovered in working with our clients that this applies even more-so when reaching out to Gay-male and lesbian markets – there are several sub-groups (there is no one-size-fits-all Gay market).

As the Music Man said, "You've Got To Know The Territory."

Use Ethnic or niche-market media. The best and most efficient means of reaching members of a sub-group in our society is through the media which specifically serves that market. Which means, if you're marketing to Hispanics, as we do often with our Miami and South Florida clients, you'll want to use Hispanic-oriented Social Networking pages, along with Hispanic media (such as Univision or el Herald), with both advertising and public/media relations outreach. We have found that this is especially important when dealing with social media, which can be very finely sliced-and-diced to deliver very specific target markets.

Culturally-Sensitive Messages. Consult with members of the targeted ethnic or niche markets to make sure you don't make an unwelcome mistake in translating your messages ("translating" for cultural nuances even if you're using English). You cannot afford to seem like an interloper or outsider – your marketing messages (especially those in the increasingly vital social networking field) must be right on-target, or they will ring false and do you no good – they may even hurt.

Culturally-Sensitive Response. If you're marketing to a Hispanic market, make sure you phone receptionist and patient-care staff can speak Spanish ... or make other arrangements. Some years ago, we helped an Egyptian-born doctor market his Medical Practice into the heavily Arabic market in Dearborn Michigan. We placed ads in, among other places, an Arabic-language newspaper published in Detroit.

They offered to translate the ad, but we asked them not to – the doctor's receptionist and staff did not speak Arabic, so we had to thread-the-needle and reach this market solely based on his ethnicity. However, the obvious ideal is to have staff members who can "speak the language," even if it's only the slang-language of an American sub-culture.

Create Distinctive Collaterals. If you are going to reach out to an ethnic or cultural minority, we have found in assisting our clients that it helps to create ethnically- or culturally-distinct collateral materials, such as brochures. However, this has to extend into the website – offer, on the home page, access to a specific web-page section targeting and serving the specific group you're seeking to serve. This must also apply to Social Networking – you are best served with separate social networking outreach sites and pages targeting the specific market niche.

Bottom line, there is a real opportunity to reach out to patients with certain inherited skin tones, certain lifestyle choices, or other factors. However, to do it effectively, you need to take these five steps, and always – always – show respect for the patient's ethnicity or lifestyle choices.

Section Two: Building a Medical Spa Into Your Existing Medical Practice

Tips to building a Medical Spa inside your existing Medical Practice

As a business, we have advised dozens of individual physicians, managers, and investors around the world about opening and operating medical spas. Be advised this is not easy, but here are a few suggestions

Physician – Don't Go it Alone: This is your business, but you're moving into a new area, one that isn't built around your core expertise. Medical spa consultants can help you set up and run your own medical spa, without you having to learn the hard way.

Find someone more experienced than you: The most important step is good management. Without that, people can, and have, lost everything. If you don't have good management skills, hire someone from outside the medical world. We get calls from interested physicians, investors and businesses around the world and we take the time to talk to them all for free. Successful businesses will be happy to talk to you and give you some advice.

Franchise Med Spas: "Turnkey solutions." That's how almost everything is marketed to physicians. However, this is not the way to go, and state boards of physicians generally agree. Instead, find the right consultant, the right business manager, and create your own unique business, one that's tailor-made to integrate with your practice.

All technology is not created equal: Despite what company reps will tell you, choosing the right technology will create big differences at the end of the year. Efficacy, cost per treatment, initial costs, usage, and a long list of other considerations should go into technology decisions. This is where experienced consultants can save you tens or even hundreds of thousands of dollars.

Beware of buying used equipment from unknown sources on eBay. The up-front price may be right, but the warranty was missing, no repair-and-replacement service. Lost revenue when equipment was down more than makes up for the up-front savings.

Understand the marketplace: Medical spas are a luxury business. For most physicians, it comes as an unwelcome surprise that their new patients are more demanding. Long waits, shabby offices, poor communication, and ambivalent staff, are all in the past.

If you're touting yourself as a luxury service, you better act like one. Hire top-notch people that are service-oriented, friendly and courteous. Protocols can be taught easier than attitude.

Rein in your ego: This is business. It's not personal. If you feel you must charge twice as much as your competitors because you "deserve it," you may have to get used to having holes in your appointment book. Know your market, know your competition, and set your pricing according to what the market will bear, rather than what you think you ought to be able to make.

In this perennial down-economy, people are more astute than ever before in checking for price, as well as quality, and they're all looking for added value. If you charge more, make sure your patient receives an "added value" – and because your prospects are likely shopping for the best doctor/patient mix, provide the kinds of value that patients are looking for.

Do not use "advanced" or "laser" in your name: The number of "advanced" laser clinics is staggering. Don't do it. It's inane, overused, and bland. I actually had a physician ask me if changing his name from Advanced Laser Centers to Advanced Laser Group would get him more business.

Network with successful medical spas: Successful business owners are happy to help newcomers to the industry. We have constant dialogue with physicians and investors who are investigating the marketplace and have advised clinics on four continents. Successful medical spas will be happy to build bridges with smart businesses.

Don't look to day spas to solve your problems: Physicians hear "spa" and immediately think that day spas have the answers they're looking for.

Wrong. Most day spas can't run themselves. The average net margins for day spas are around 8%. The average physician's is around 60%. Physicians running day spas are entering a business that they know nothing about, doesn't make any money, is highly competitive, has no barriers to entry, and is rife with employee and other problems. Don't do it.

If you're going there, think about establishing a medical spa which also offers day spa services, rather than just operating a day spa – the margins are higher, and they will be more effective in generating referrals into your primary business.

Don't base your pay on commissions: Commissions sound like a great solution. You save overhead and motivate your staff to grow the business. False. Commissions are used in spas to keep overhead low. But guess what? Staff members working for commission aren't working for you. Commissions lead to overly aggressive staff, constant drama, and high employee turnover that can hurt your reputation.

Don't Gild the Lily: You may have heard that you have to spend a fortune to "build out" your clinic. Nope. You don't have to start with treatment tables that have your clinics name embossed on them. Spend all your money before you open and you won't be able to spend it where you'll really need it... getting patients in the seats.

Instead, you need a solid and reasonable budget and pro-forma, and you have enough money set aside for marketing – up to 20 percent of desired revenue for a start-up, and around 7-10 percent for a well-established business. This is what you need to drive sufficient patients into your practice to pay for your impressively built-out clinic.

Stay lean: Physicians practice medicine based on science. You don't need to offer pedicures and you don't know anything about them anyway. Stick to the basics.

Plunging Into Something New

If you plan to add a medical-spa component to your Medical Practice, here are some things to consider

Running a successful Medical Practice is no simple task. It takes dedication from you and your employees to deliver your products or services effectively and profitably. This article will cover what you should consider if you are planning to open a medical spa alongside your existing Medical Practice.

I assume that you already have an established Medical Practice based on a robust infrastructure that includes an actionable business plan, a solid patient roster, and qualified employees. Now, you perceive an opportunity to branch out and open a medical spa.

A few of the natural synergies between the two businesses are:

- The medical spa may become a source for new medical patients.

- Medical patients may become a source for new medical-spa patients.

- Medical-spa procedures can be performed by other health care professionals under your supervision. (Check your particular state's regulations on this.) Thus, you are able to obtain more income without actually having to perform the procedures.

- Additional retail opportunities present themselves through the medical spa.

Perhaps there is an extra exam room in your existing Medical Practice that may be used for this new venture, or at least for the start-up. Before you know it, a new business is born. Nevertheless, please wait before taking the plunge. Important planning work needs to be done.

Look Before You Leap

Before embarking on this powerfully exciting opportunity to expand your Medical Practice, use caution. Be sure to ask your current patients if they would be interested in obtaining medical-spa services from you and at your location; and if so, which types of services they would want.

Other considerations to be resolved beforehand include developing a separate financial infrastructure. Even if your medical spa will be located in an additional exam room in your Medical Practice, you should have a separate accounting function for that business that properly identifies its expenses and tracks its profitability to ensure that adding the new treatments or services is indeed profitable for your Medical Practice. One of the pitfalls of adding new treatments to existing medical practices is that most owners never know if they are profitable.

Although your practice and medical spa may have the same owner, they are very different businesses. To realize their full scope of profits and benefits, they should be treated as such from the outset.

If you wish, you could overlap some of your businesses' back-office functions. For example, you can centralize the call center and appointment-setting function, as well as bookkeeping, accounting, and purchasing. This way, you will achieve economies of scale without affecting the way the two businesses appear to the public.

Build that Diving Board

Once you decide that you are primed to launch into the medical-spa business, be sure to create the vital step in your road map to success: a business plan. Think of your business plan as your plan for success. It will help you navigate around the potential business barriers, recognize opportunities, and remind you of your organization's strengths and weakness.

I cannot stress this point enough: Every business – even a medical spa – needs a business plan. The process of creating a business plan should help you avoid costly mistakes and the loss of time and money. It will also provide a blueprint for management staff to follow.

The first consideration in this venture is your medical spa's location. Ideally, it should be located in a separate office space from your existing Medical Practice to enable the patient to feel that he or she has entered a "spa." The aesthetic first impression is very important. Your medical spa should have the look and feel of an upscale soothing environment.

Select a location in a more "retail"-like area that has easy access, adequate parking, good lighting at night, and good security. An upscale shopping center is a good choice, but a medical building or hospital – which is associated with medical care – is not. Since a medical spa is a wellness and aesthetic business, its location should not conjure up medical or hospital imagery.

The more visibility the better. A busy shopping center with lots of foot traffic will bring many prospects to your door, and your advertising costs will be less than they might otherwise be.

This new business should also have its own branding, including a different name and logo than your Medical Practice. Your name, of course, should be prominently displayed as medical director, along with your medical credentials. When creating your brand, identify the market niche you want to serve and create a menu of services that reflects it in your style and the treatments you offer.

One ... Two ... Three ... Jump!

When starting a new venture like this, it is best to begin the public relations and marketing work 2 to 3 months before you plan to open it. At this time, it is a good idea to establish yourself as an expert in certain medical treatments and let your community know about you. Consider hiring a public relations professional to help you leverage your expertise in the minds and "wallets" of your potential patients.

It is also best to hire the person who will manage the business at this time so that you can focus your time on revenue-building activities like treating patients. Initially, this person should research the marketplace by obtaining service menus and prices from your competitors. This information will then help you create your own menu and pricing structure.

Likewise, start developing your private-label product line at this time so that it will be ready when you open your medical spa. Since a medical spa is a retail business, selling skin care products will add significant profit potential. Patients may purchase products on a monthly basis whether or not they will be coming in for treatments.

In addition, your particular private-label products cannot be purchased over the Internet in general—but they can be purchased on your own Web site, which keeps patients looking at your brand. With your menu and skin care lines, you can effectively cross-sell and up-sell packages of multiple treatments and products to use at home to enhance their benefits.

The increasing number of medical spas that have opened in recent years has successfully intermingled medical with noninvasive spa procedures, Medical spas may in fact be the most cost-effective referral service for elective medical. If your medical spa is successful on its own, you should also enjoy of the benefits of crossover patients.

With proper planning from the beginning, this venture can bring great rewards in professional satisfaction and profits.

Section Three: Marketing Your MedSpa

Your Cosmetic Medical Spa Roadmap to Success

It has been said that success is a journey. And, no journey is complete without a roadmap. Just like any road trip, there are some quintessential considerations that must be part of your planning and execution process.

I have logged more than a million miles in working with medical spas around the country. I help them by building a program and creating just the right roadmaps to help cosmetic medical spa entrepreneurs navigate their way to a successful business destination.

This takes entrepreneurs through the important steps necessary to navigate the path to a successful cosmetic medical spa launch and the steps necessary to sustain and grow their business ventures.

Just like with a road trip, how will you know if you reached your destination if you never outlined one? A strategic plan is just that – a roadmap for what you plan to accomplish, and the various tactics that you will implement to arrive at that goal.

This is the most important first step towards your journey.

You cannot skip this step, and you must spend incredible energy and resources – thought and time – creating your document. You will turn to your strategic plan repeatedly during the implementation and growth stage of your new business venture.

Whether you choose to do this on your own, select one of several great software programs that helps to guide you through writing a business plan, or you hire a consultant, these essential elements must be part of your roadmap to success.

Strategic Planning

You will need a Feasibility overview outlining the business potential, if you are seeking financing. You will also need an Executive Summary that captures the key components of your strategic planning document.

Mission and Vision Statement

Do not skip this step.

Writing this helps you to determine your unique selling proposition (USP) –what separates you from the perceived competition to give you competitive advantage, and to remind you and your staff of the underlying motivation for your business venture.

These two different documents differ.

Together they provide direction for the business by focusing your attention on doing things day-to-day to accomplish your mission, while taking steps to pursue your vision of the future – your long-term business intent. A **mission** statement explains why you exist today and/or what you are doing to pursue your **vision** of the future.

- **Mission Statement** is a statement of the organization's purpose – what it wants to accomplish in a larger environment. Writing a formal company mission statement is not easy. A clear mission statement acts as an invisible hand that guides people in the organization so that they can work independently and yet collectively toward overall organizational goals.

- **The Vision Statement** describes the future: where you are going or where you want to go. A solid vision, documented as the Vision Statement, creates commitment and understanding.

  It enables your team to focus on the future, and it enables others who read it to understand how the top of the organization visualizes the future. Initially it is a dream that with the right plan, personnel, commitment, and execution can come to fruition.

The words should also reflect the values the organization actually lives rather than those it believes it *ought to* live by. Some organizations frame the vision statement and display it in an area frequented by their customers.

SWOTT analysis

You can conduct your own SWOTT analysis, a variation on the traditional SWOT analysis that includes all-important Trends. SWOTT stands for strengths, weaknesses, opportunities, threats, and trends. This is a very important step to ensure that your business is ready to enter the marketplace and excel in our elect geographic location.

To carry out a SWOTT Analysis, consider the following:

- **Strengths:** Consider your business venture strengths from your own point of view and from the point of view of the people you deal with. Be realistic.

  Are you able to differentiate yourself from the competition based on your strengths? Can you use this to create competitive advantage that can be sustained? This is called as sustainable competitive advantage and means that what you have created will take significant time for any potential competitors to catch up to your product and/or service offerings.

- **Weaknesses:** These should be viewed from both an internal and external perspective. This may be tough, but do be sure to be realistic to uncover any issues that can and should be averted.

- **Opportunities:** Examine what you wrote in your strengths list and look at each for potential opportunities, e.g., you have amazing expertise with a particular laser or procedure. Conversely, examine your weaknesses list to see if there may be some procedures or treatments that should be deleted from your menu of services, and the impact of eliminating them.

- **Threats:** Although this may sound like the worst of the elements, truly it is not. It can be a very positive and fruitful endeavor. Consider what threatens your business opportunities from becoming realities. This will help you understand what needs to be done to eliminate the threats to ensure that the opportunities listed have a great opportunity to thrive!

- **Trends:** Forecasting trends is an essential element to any business venture. Being ready with the solution, treatment, or procedure as it becomes popular will set you up for being the go-to medispa for the latest and greatest in medical spa care.

Administrative Efficiencies

These essential elements create the backbone of daily operations.

They include selecting the right:

- Accounting software

- Patient management software

Choose software that includes inventory and product control solutions, a general menu of services with descriptions, a list of equipment needed with prices, staff requirements and job descriptions, start-up cost projections, cash flow projections, and an overview of marketing strategies.

Financial Projections

Ensure that you your business venture is well capitalized.

Many businesses fail because they are undercapitalized. Take great effort in assessing your financial projections, your Return on Investment (ROI), and your break even points.

Be sure to have a two-year cash flow projection, both real and stretch targets.

Pay close attention to your metrics and ratios to ensure that they are both reasonable. For example, your rent should be approximately five percent of projected gross revenue; your marketing budget should be calculated at around fifteen percent of revenue.

Establish the proper ownership structure for your business

Because of the potential liability of a medical spa business, you will almost surely want to form a business entity that provides personal liability protection, which shields your personal assets from business debts and claims. Consult with an attorney that specializes in this field to determine what is right for your situation.

Check with your state board of medical examiners to see who can administer the following treatments in your states and plan your staff accordingly.

Also, ensure that all medical or cosmetology personnel are properly licensed within the state in which they will be practicing.

Determine if the medical director must be onsite, and establish appropriate compensation.

If you own a spa that is transitioning to a medical spa, or you are an entrepreneur starting a medical spa, you will need to check with your state laws regarding physician involvement in medical spa ownership and management. Consult your attorney, but in most states, the best way to structure the physician's compensation is to establish a management services agreement.

Obtain the proper insurance coverage

It is critical that you carry adequate malpractice insurance for the medical director, the facility, and for the practitioners. Look for insurance brokerage firms that provide special attention to the needs of medical spa owners, including offering policies for clinical treatments.

They can assist you in making decision about coverage for your medical spa.

The cost of medical spa liability insurance is determined by the spa's revenue, the number of client visits, the type of procedures, and the provider.

As the spa's revenues and procedure levels increase, the insurance premium rise, too.

Premium costs are about $15,000 to $25,000 for new companies.

You can search the Internet for your state department of insurance and find authorized malpractice providers in your area.

Hire an architect/designer

Assuming you have already chosen the location for your medical spa (I recommend a minimum of 1600-2500 sq. ft.), it is critical that you properly plan and decorate your space. Ideally, a medical spa should have a relaxing and luxurious environment. This is a high-end retail business and clients expect to be pampered and serviced properly.

Keep in mind that selecting an architect/designer with industry experience can actually save you money in the long run. They will already know the specific requirements for your project and you will not need to pay for their learning curve. They can guide you as to the proper number of treatment rooms, non-revenue generating space, and client flow.

Select a reputable contractor/builder

Although many architects have contractors that they work with, you may need to hire one in order to turn your plans into reality. A good general contractor then hires and, supervises all subcontractors, including, hydraulics, electrical and mechanical engineers, as well as flooring, painting, and carpentry professionals.

Be sure to obtain a contract before any work begins and make sure your builder applies for the appropriate permits required, including building or fire permits. Keep in touch throughout the process and speak up about any discrepancies with the contract.

Create a winning name

You will need a good name for your medical spa. It should reflect what clients could expect when they walk through the door. A good name should be brandable. Be sure you have selected something distinctive and something that people can easily recall. Along with a great name, do not forget to develop a brand tag line. This is a great way to distinguish your unique offerings from your competitors.

Once you choose a name, you will need to register it with the appropriate authorities depending on how your business is structured. Check with your attorney for the specific details on this. Also, remember to pick a website domain name and register it on any Internet registration site such as www.register.com.

Choose a graphic designer

Branding your medical spa is critical to its success. A good graphic designer will design a logo and color scheme that includes your name and possibly a logo or symbol to reflect your identity. This logo should he used in all of your marketing collateral including, all of your brand identify, stationary, website, brochures, and business cards.

Select your retail product line(s)

Decide whether to go with name brand, private label or both. There are literally hundreds 0f name brand skin care lines available today and most have excellent marketing literature, packaging, samples, and collateral materials. You can develop a list of possible candidates by asking other physicians or businesses for recommendations as well as searching the internet, industry, or trade publications, or going to trade shows.

However, most all of these name brand lines will be available at other businesses in your area or over the internet. Not only will this competition limit your retail product sales, but call impact your repeat client business.

Choosing a private label product line gives you a competitive edge. Using your name and logo on the products enhances your brand and image. Also, clients perceive that they can only get these products at your spa and because private label products are less costly to you, the profit margins are usually higher. You will have to develop your own collateral materials and training but the impact on your overall business makes it worth it.

Do be careful to identify products that are unique and not generally available at your competitors or on a website. Offering products that are medically based helps create traffic flow to your spa.

Customers will seek out your facility to purchase specific products that are only offered at medically supervised facilities. As a result, you will have a chance to introduce them to your full spectrum of cosmetic medical spa services.

Develop a comprehensive treatment menu – along with signature services

The first step is to select your professional product line. This is sometimes called back bar products because they are products used by the professional, for example, TCA peels.
Once the product lines are selected, then you can create your detailed menu of services.

Try to give each treatment or service a catchy name and then write a brief description that includes price, time.

An aesthetic medical spa menu should include at least the following categories: Medical facials, Injectables, Microdermabrasion, Facial rejuvenation, peels, Laser and light treatments, anti-aging medicine, Body Care, Massage Therapy, and make-up.

Do consider creating package pricing. When your patients elect to take advantage of a series of treatments, they end up with the best results, and you end up with happy patients. It's a win-win for you both.

Provide patient financing

Cost remains the number one reason why people do not schedule procedures or even come in for consultation. Providing your patients with a financing option can significantly increase your chance for success by making your services accessible to a wider clientele. Your consultation specialists are able to close more sales by helping clients fit the cost of the procedures into their monthly budget.

You can also sell more large packages and service series in advance.

CareCredit, a division of GE Capital Consumer Finance, currently offers a revolving line of credit with no interest, exclusively for physicians and medical spas. Healthcare Finance Direct is another Medical Practice-supporting patient finance tool. They both have comprehensives range of payment plans for your clients. Credit can be applied for at home or in your office, with credit decisions provided in seconds. You receive payment within just a few business days, regardless of how the client pays. Both systems are easy to use and integrate into your existing payment options.

Selecting tile right Furniture, Fixtures, and Equipment for your medical spa

Technology is constantly changing. Don't put the cart before the horse. Know what your needs will be-- both spatially and service wise-- before committing to equipment purchases. For this reason, the best time to negotiate your equipment contracts is just a few months before you open for business.

In addition to lasers and Microdermabrasion machines, you will need treatment beds, carts, magnifying lamps, and more for each treatment room.

You will also need furniture for the consultation room, waiting area, check-in and checkout area and office. Do not forget cash drawers, receipt printers, a credit card machine, brochure and business card holders and file cabinets.

Be sure to invest in a good software program designed for medical spas. There are many good ones available.

Look for the following key areas: appointment book capacity, payroll management, POS system, inventory control system, and a good management reporting system. And, no doubt, you are well aware of the nationwide movement towards electronic medical record adoption. This will affect your business as well.

There are many great companies that offering electronic medical record solutions. Use care in identifying just the right solution that meets your needs.

You will also need a laundry list of supplies for each treatment room, for example, linens, bowls, tissues, wipes, gloves, etc. A medical spa consultant can help you with refining the furniture, fixtures, and equipment, and other supplies specific to your project.

Hire the Right Staff – ones with The Right Stuff

The right staff starts with the right resume search. Begin your search about three to four months before you are set to launch your business. Write job descriptions for each position you intend to hire. Carefully screen your applicants using this as a tool. Place ads in the newspaper and on the Internet. Screen the resumes, interview candidates by phone and then bring the top two to three in for face-to-face interviews. Bring in the spa director or manager at least two months before your planned opening date.

Design a compensation plan that includes commissions and incentives for meeting targets and goals and make sure your compensation plan does not represent more than 50 percent of your total cost of sales.

Have a plan for who will perform each treatment and train them accordingly. Also, develop an employee manual outlining your company policies on everything from housekeeping arid staff meetings to vacation and sick days allowed. You may also want to consider employee and independent contractor agreements to outline compensation, grounds for dismissal and non-compete clauses.

Create an Actionable Marketing Plan

A marketing plan starts with identifying the amount of resources you will dedicate to marketing your business. A good start is to estimate fifteen percent of your first year projected gross earnings, and use this as your marketing budget. Do take into consideration the unique circumstances of your organization and adjust your budget accordingly.

For example, if you are in a large city hub where competition is fierce, plan on a more generous marketing budget allocation.

Include strategy and tactics for at least your first year of operation.

Proven marketing tactics for cosmetic medical spas include, marketing brochures, direct mail, electronic and print advertising, public relations, community relations, and special events. Do not overlook the potential of getting involved in your community through the chamber of commerce, and business networking groups. A great way to jumpstart your business is to affiliate with industry related organizations, such as the International Spa Association.

Create an operating manual

Many cosmetic medical spas tend to skip this step because by the time they get to this point they are either too busy or too exhausted to put it together. This is your guidebook to success. Be sure your operating manual includes the following sections that include administrative policies and procedures, inventory and retail procedures, treatment protocols, client flow and etiquette, patient consultation forms, home care prescription forms, and staff job descriptions.

Ensure your medical spa is OSHA and HIPAA compliant

OSHA stands for Occupational Safety and Health Administration and their guidelines are enforced for every business nationwide. All employees including new hires must be trained prior to being assigned to a task that could put him or her at any safety or health risk. Additionally, all employees must be aware of your facility's fire and emergency plans. To find out information about the requirements for your business, go to www.osha.gov.

The Health Insurance Portability and Accountability Act (HIPAA) has completely changed the way healthcare businesses handle private customer/client information. For medical spas, this means that you will need HIPAA Compliant procedures in place, even before you open the door to new clients.

For more information, http://www.ems.hhs.gov/home/regsguidance.asp.

Create a winning advisory team

This is the time to call in all the great experts in their respective fields to provide you with the right advice, at the right time, and in the right place so that you can avoid some potential business pitfalls. Set to work now to build your team of experts that should include a specialized attorney, CPA, and cosmetic medical spa consultant. Why go through all of the effort to set up your business without the benefit of expert wisdom and sage advice.

Now is the time to take a very proactive, strategic, and serious approach to creating the business of your dreams. It is possible, and it is possible because you now have the essential elements to create your roadmap to success. Do remember that each step is important and that the time you spend carefully executing each part will reward you with the financial and professionals dividends that make the journey of success so very great.

Going Medical with Your Spa

You may not realize it, but today, you are sitting on the edge.

With 30% of the nation's population among the Baby Boomers – a group with enormous spending power *and* the desire to defy age – procedures to help stave off Father Time are in growing demand. But that understates it. These procedures, along with related products and services, are expected to become the next trillion dollar industry. And as the proud owner of a spa, you are on the edge of it all.

But you're not quite sitting inside, which is where the windfall will be. That's because spas tend to offer what I called "related products and services." These are *part* of the equation, but they're not the whole story, and they're not the basis for the story.

It's true that a spa can offer someone a lot for feeling better and maybe going up against Time in a jabbing match — but it's never going to score a knock-out. As Baby Boomers age, they're going after the knock-out for one of two reasons: 1) they have the money to spend, and the first area of concern will be to hang on to what they've enjoyed so much: their youth; and 2) economic and population realities are going to keep more people working longer, and a youthful vigor is becoming more critical in a person's later years.

With a spa, you are able to assist in this trend and no doubt have some success. But by converting your spa into a medical spa, you are more likely to help yourself to this new pot of gold. *How do you do it?* Glad you asked. Here are some of the critical steps.

Structure is Critical

First, it's important to know that every state has different laws regarding how you can run a medical spa. For instance, a number of states have laws against doctors and non-doctors running a business together. If this is the case where you operate your spa, you'll need to structure your business accordingly ... like by *renting space to a doctor* for in-house procedures. Another option would be to create certain partnerships in which a doctor refers patients to you for pre- and post-operative care and instruction, while you refer patients to this doctor for any medical procedures.

Because every state has its own requirements, it would be valuable for you to find an appropriate health care spa consultant who will work with your lawyer or recommend one. Having someone like this on hand will help you make sure that you consider all the necessary changes and implement them in the right order.

Because of your new structure, you're also going to need a new business plan. This plan should make special note of the differences between a spa and a medical spa. In the case of anything medical, clients are going to expect more quality and more professionalism.

Your décor, your marketing efforts, and every kind of interaction with people should aim at this updated image. All of this may even call for a new *or revised* name for your business. If you already have strong name recognition, keeping the name and stylization (i.e., store-front lettering, logos, etc.) may be a better bet than changing the name altogether ... but you'll want to modify it to showcase your new medical offerings.

The Best Possible Staff

Going medical means two things for personnel: 1) training current staff; 2) hiring on new staff. The first of these is important because, in most cases, spa personnel are used to a more casual atmosphere than a medical spa requires. Depending on the way you're already doing things, you may need to train for a new approach to answering phones, greeting clients as they walk in, helping customers to fill in medical forms, and so on. You may also need to upgrade your dress code.

Also, customers won't just be calling in to ask the front desk about hours anymore. They'll have more concerns and very specific questions about medical procedures they'll be going through. You should plan for more phone time, which means shifting certain responsibilities away from your receptionist or hiring on someone specifically for these calls.

This person needs to be well-educated about the various procedures you offer, and in fact, the more your staff knows about what you provide, the better equipped they are to assist clients. It would be a good idea to offer services at-cost — or even for free, for training purposes – to your staff so they can speak to clients from experience.

New staff will at least include a couple of nurses, for administering injections and helping with other simple procedures, depending on state laws. And ideally you will have a doctor on site any time there are medically-related procedures being performed, or at least a phone call away, *even if the doctor is not overseeing the procedure.*

This way, if there is any kind of mishap, you have someone immediately available to take over or help with the situation. Whether the doctor is needed on-site or by phone is dictated by state law. It's important to know your state laws and to keep doctors as accessible as possible.

New Marketing for a New Business

Finally, you can't shift from spa to medical spa without shifting your approach to marketing as well. As I mentioned, you'll want to step everything up in professionalism; if you have sort of a creative or daring slant to your current advertising, it's probably time to begin a new campaign. In print ads, time to start using more traditional fonts; color ads may want a medical green or blue incorporated somehow. You need to build a medical image.

But print ads will only take you so far. One primary thing to remember: the media is your best friend. Get them to love you and your business will thrive. Perhaps invite them to a pre-opening "media day" with complimentary gift certificates. Offer your new medical treatments at cost. If you're as good as you'd better be in this business, you can generate some terrific and widespread word-of-mouth this way.

The media can also help you out if you're helping out the public. Offer free seminars that educate, explaining the different ways people can fend off Father Time; you do not want to specifically promote your business in this kind of seminar, but you will certainly want yourself prominently displayed as the sponsor.

You can also generally get media attention any time you are supporting or giving back to the community in some way, perhaps by holding fund raisers. If you give the media at least three weeks' advance notice, they can give your seminar or events free coverage, bringing more people in and branding your name and logo in their minds.

Finally, you may still offer spa services, but now you're something more – a new business really. This gives you the chance to offer a Grand Re-Opening. Newspaper or radio ads offering substantial discounts on the new medical procedures, or even "bring a friend and get half off" coupons (to expand your current clientele) are a great way to start things off with a bang. After all … you've invested a lot in your new medical spa.

Now it's time to reap the rewards.

Ten Keys to Launching and Maintaining a 'Stand Out From the Competition' Successful Medical Spa

The core competency of a super successful next generation Aesthetic Medical Spa owner blends the medical quest for excellence with the newest, best of breed beauty treatments and services.

Staying ahead of the "power curve" and developing a can and will do no matter what tries to derail you attitude, is the essential character-defining attribute of the successful medical spa entrepreneur.

Do you have what it takes to be a leader in this ultra hot market space?

One physician that is happy with her decision is Camille Cash, MD; a Houston based Plastic Surgeon who has expanded her Medical Practice to include medical spa services.

Explaining why she made the transition, Dr. Cash said, "It's my opinion that patients would prefer to see their plastic surgeon for these non-invasive aesthetic procedures. Medical Grade spa services offer the opportunity to provide additional non-surgical services to infuse cash into the practice. These are also procedures that provide a lot of patients' satisfaction without significant risk."

Are you ready to expand your Medical Practice service offerings and provide your patients with services they are currently seeking from other sources?

Are you ready to convert your patients into medical spa service clients?

If the answer is "yes," if you are indeed ready to expand into the world of Cosmetic Medical Spas, here are some key concepts to embrace to help you launch and maintain a "Stand out from the Competition" successful medical spa component to your existing Medical Practice, or standalone facility.

Medical Spas Are Retail Businesses, Requiring a Focused Commitment to a Robust ROI

Do you understand the myths and realities of medical spa economics? You need to ensure that you are ready to commit adequate financial resources to your business endeavor. You need to evaluate all the various areas of financial commitment and then be certain you have the financial "war chest" to create your medical spa from concept to flourishing business. Be sure that you do not overlook the importance of starting with the basics that all business owners respect, everything from the building or medical spa location to training and staff development.

You will want to have legal and compliance professionals review your business plan specific to your own local and state regulations, and privacy laws. These laws can affect the set-up of your medical spa and its services and dictate that your staff be trained to use discretion concerning treatments and/or how medical charts are stored or verbally discussed Consider what professionals you will need on your team to ensure success, for example, business managers and lawyers, marketing, and public relations professionals.

Remember that your marketing and public relations program must be in place and actionable well before you open your medical spa doors!

Environmental Scan – knowing your Competition Inside Out

Just because you have a great concept and a well-funded business plan does not guarantee your success. You must first evaluate the demographics of the location that you have designated for your medical spa. Honestly, this is frequently the make or break research assignment that many business entrepreneurs fail to include in their medical spa development decision-making process. A word of strong caution: Know your potential marketplace to ensure that "if you build it, they will come!"

You can do this by conducting by using primary research – some ad hoc focus groups and by surfing the Internet for secondary research. For example, you can identify the socio-economic make-up of your proposed location by gathering information from the government through the U.S.

Census Bureau (www.census.gov), the city clerk's office, or real estate agencies, and chambers of commerce. If you plan to use professional consultants, they can provide this analysis as part of their services.

Knowing your competition inside and out is essential to ensure that you do not create medical spa that has to take business away from potential competitors. Instead, you want to carve out your own unique niche that may attract an untapped market for your special services. Be sure to check out the competition thoroughly. How? Start by visiting their websites. Look at staff credentials, number of staff members, services offered, and fees charged. Make extensive phone calls to gather menus of everything offered in the area.

Then make personal visits, or have trusted colleagues schedule a variety of treatments. Remember that the nicest website may be just window dressing for a ho-hum operation. Once you have checked out the competition, you will know what services they offer. To be successful, provide alternative services – give the public what it is currently lacking.

You must make your medical spa unique. How? You create a niche market for yourself. Find and fulfill a need that will make you stand out in the crowd, no matter how great the competition. You might decide to specialize – focusing on acne treatments, age management, or anti-aging medicine. Alternatively, you might decide to have a "men-only" facility. Let your uniqueness and your passion be your guide.

To Serve and Make Beautiful – Your Service Mantra

Often medical spas miss the mark because they focus solely on the variety and quantity of services. To ensure a successful business result, think first about putting "service" into the services – or adopt the "quality is supreme mantra." Even though you will create a tailored service menu to meet and exceed the expectations of your customers, be sure that the most important part of any service is the **"serv"** part.

Ask tough questions of your staff. Beyond the technical ability and/or treatment services and technology to perform the requested service, they need to be fully empowered to provide the highest level of quality service to each client.

Why is this important? Excellent client experience will primarily create a loyal following, and create the foundation for your much need Word of Mouth Marketing (WOMM) program to gain you additional **market share!**

Konstantin Vasyukevich, MD a facial plastic surgeon practicing in New York City offers non-surgical services such as Botox and dermal fillers in his Medical Practice.

Dr. Vasyukevich explains, "My patients are used to receiving the utmost in professional and technically superior surgical services. They expect and we deliver the same very high quality service to our non-surgical patients as we provide to our plastic surgery patients. This is our mission and we have an unwavering commitment to ensure that we deliver on this promise."

Designing the Winning Menu of Services

Any successful restaurateur knows the importance of creating a winning menu that continues to delight, anticipate, and tantalize the taste buds. Take a lesson from your favorite gourmet inspired restaurant to help you formulate the menu of services that will distinguish your medical spa.

How do you jumpstart the menu creation process? Think in terms of tried and true services and combine with a dazzling array of up-to-the-minute, must have now service offerings. Today's medical spa client is very informed and proactively seeks just the right destination for their beauty enhancement procedures.

They know the result they are looking for and it is up to you and your staff to help guide them to the right treatment options, services, and procedures to help them attain their goals. You can stay up to date with trends by subscribing to industry trade publications, joining anti-aging associations, getting on the mail list for various industry companies and associations, and exchanging information internally from the spa side to the medical side and vice versa.

You must determine your range of services. Will you provide general services that appeal to a diverse market-driven clientele or will you specialize to appeal to a niche consumer-base?

You must know this before you set out to write your menu of services. Start with these questions: what is the medical spa specialty that will best meet the needs of my prospective customers and match my professional expertise? Will it be more profitable to serve general needs? Alternatively, will I create a more substantial medical spa business expansion by specializing in one or two target markets?

Perhaps you will want to specialize in men's services. In this case, you would want to offer laser hair removal for the back and face. On the other hand, will you want to specialize in the ethnic market? Do you know what services are most sought after by this sub-group?

Alternatively, do you want to provide a general medical spa service menu that features treatments such as peels, lymphatic drainage, microdermabrasion, or laser hair removal?

Location, Location, Location
Inside of Your Medical Spa

We are not talking here about where in the city, state, or nation you decide to build your medical spa. Instead, what is very important to the client is where they are receiving their treatments and services once they have entered your building. You would be surprised at how this plays a large role in your future visits from the client and their desire to provide you with Word of Mouth Marketing.

Whether you are revamping current office space, or building the facility from the ground up, two essential location-related areas need immediate attention.

Creating a spa like environment is important for the client. It helps them separate the fact that this is not an illness visit, but instead, elective services visit to improve their appearance. To assess you cosmetic medical spa "patient oasis," check to see if you have created space that is comfortable for the client. With a medical spa service offering, you need to ensure that the spa is not medically or exam room-like in appearance and décor.

This includes ensuring that the room is quasi-sound proof. Then, consider the message. What is the level of ambiance and uniqueness that you are trying to convey at your medical spa? Unlike a medical office, your medical spa should not have a medical office feel. Clients coming to your medical spa already feel great. They just want to enhance their appearance and wellness outlook.

Second, when considering your interior location, be sure that all of your rooms are multipurpose. You may not need to add extra space if every treatment room is multi-functional. Your staff also needs to be cross-trained. The receptionist or appointment booker needs to be just as conversant and knowledgeable about your service menu as the physicians themselves. However, that does not mean they dispense medical advice to the caller.

In-house satisfaction assessment surveys about your menu and staff performance are a good way to gauge satisfaction levels. Better to fill your client's needs by adding treatments than to have them look for the elsewhere.

Prepare Your Office

You will make your choices about equipment, design, and décor based on your research. You are now in the business of pampering as well as practicing medicine, so you should aim for a soothing nonmedical environment.

Remember, some of the people coming to your new facility will be "clients" as opposed to "patients." They are coming to de-stress. They are looking for the relaxing "spa" aspect of the medical spa, as opposed to the sterile atmosphere of a doctor's office. Changing your décor and the ambiance of your facility does not have to be dramatic.

Something as subtle as using earth-tone colors on a wall or replacing the Musak with some New Age CD's goes a long way toward modifying your atmosphere. By the way, that subtle change in environment works wonders for your staff, too – they will be more productive and happier in a more pleasant atmosphere.

Make sure that when clients walk through your doors they are immediately impressed and delighted with the environment you've created.

It is like meeting someone for the first time first impressions really do count! Pay close attention to everything in the waiting room and at the receptionist's desk. Make sure that all your marketing collateral materials are organized, up-to-date, and create a consistent brand image.

The first impression here sets the stage for your prospective client from prospect to patient. Make a concerted effort to do this first step right. You may want to seek a professional consultant for tips.

You also want to ensure that customer service is an action and not merely a motto. Assess truthfully the public's perception of your cosmetic medical spa. Is your office exceedingly customer service friendly? Analyze such areas as waiting time (should be minimal). It is also helpful to have a separate "holding" or waiting area that is peaceful and relaxing.

Here perhaps you could make healthy teas and water available. Spa goers feel more at ease in a relaxing and private setting, so do what you can to create this environment for your clientele.

Also, most physicians that offer both medical services and cosmetic medical centers are most successful when they can at least create two separate waiting areas so that ill patients are not sitting with the spa service seekers. You may also want to consider what the Miami Institute has found to be a great benefit for their clients.

They have created a VIP waiting room that leads to a separate entrance into a VIP holding room.

Think special, think privacy, think relaxing and tranquil – key elements that will attract and maintain a loyal customer-baser.

Selecting the Right Equipment and Distributor

Buy or Lease? Choosing equipment depends on your menu of services and the specific demographics – what the potential clientele is seeking in their particular neighborhood. What essential is that you realize that this is not an "emotional" buy. You need to do your homework to ensure you make the right purchases, for the right reasons, and for the right service and treatment protocols. For this reason, never make a buying decision at a trade show, and most importantly, never make a purchase decision because you feel under pressure.

Follow the following powerful suggestions to focus on acquiring just the right equipment. You are not ready to identify your equipment needs until you create a financial projection, a demographic review, and a tailored menu of services. Here is a checklist to get you started on the right course of action.

First, you will need to decide if you are going to make an equipment purchase investment, or forestall purchasing in lieu of some fine equipment leasing options. This is one decision that strongly favors going the leasing route since technology is rapidly changing so you the important option of constantly upgrading your equipment.

Then, identify an equipment supplier that has many years of experience in the medical or spa industry. Collaborating with the right distributor will reap great rewards for many years. Beautiful Forever Aesthetic Business Consulting is a great resource for helping guide you to just the right suppliers and vendors.

You'll want an equipment supplier that offers a large selection, highly trained staff, outstanding customer service, and competitive pricing – just call their 800 number and see I someone is waiting to assist you. Make sure the company has a good support/service staff that will be able to replace equipment within 24 hours should there be a problem.

You create what can become a lifelong partnership when you choose a supplier, so do your homework The Right Supplier – This is a crucial decision. The right supplier will become your trusted partner, supporter, and go-to source. Don't make price alone the deciding factor when narrowing the field of potential supply partners. While you may find that some distributors have significantly lower prices – they may be carrying overstocks or discontinued products.

Moreover, they may not offer a wide range of services and support.

Staff of Experts: Be sure that your supplier has been in business for several years and has a highly trained and experienced staff. These folks make it their business to know equipment and take pride in providing the best service.

Selection: A professional spa business development organization can help you select equipment that fits your budget and allows you to perform the treatments on your menu. The best distributors offer a large selection to choose from, saving you time and effort. You do not have to do exhaustive research and make calls to several different companies. Utilize the distributor's knowledge and expertise. It is their business to offer innovative solutions that meet your needs. You need to focus on providing your patients with a truly unique experience!

Logistics: After you have made your choices, your Distributor Partner will make certain that you get what you need when you need it. Because different pieces of equipment may have to be shipped from different locations (some even around the world), you want to select a Distributor Partner that has experience in working out the logistics and agreeing on suitable timelines.

Unrealistic Timelines? Your Distributor Partner will provide you with options and work with you to develop solutions.

Specs and Installation Information: One of the most important components in setting up treatment rooms and a medical spa is accurate installation information, which your Distributor Partner can provide. Obtain required information in advance for architects and designers. Because this information often goes through several hands during the design/planning phase and can get lost, an electronic format for documents is great – they can be stored and printed as needed.

Information When You Need It: Your Distributor Partner should be able to provide Warranties and Operating Manuals to you for each piece of equipment you purchase. Lost your information? Or did you accidentally throw out important paperwork that was in the packing box? Your Distributor Partner should have an 800 number where a customer service rep can easily accommodate your requests whether you need information by post, fax, or email.

Or do you have a question about your account? No problem. Your Distributor partner should have knowledgeable staff (and the infrastructure needed, i.e. data based IT support) to answer your questions.

Having Equipment Problems? Need a Replacement Part? Your Distributor Partner should have technical service reps to help you troubleshoot problems to make sure that you are using the equipment properly, and that it has been adequately cleaned and maintained. Frequently, minor problems can be corrected immediately via the phone. If needed, your Distributor Partner should be able to provide you with replacement parts or have the ability to make needed repairs in a timely manner.

Select the Right Staff

This is the time to take heed and study some retail success stories.

Nordstrom's for example has made its mark on a fine tradition of customer service. Think carefully about your staff to ensure that each staff member is able to create a customer-centric approach to meeting and exceeding client expectations. This is a far different set of services that you are providing in your Medical Practice where mostly the patients' services are covered in part or full by medical healthcare insurance coverage.

Since most of your clients in the medical spa component will be cash paying clientele, they can afford to be very discriminating about where and from whom they receive their aesthetic enhancement services. Do what you can right from the start to create a staff culture of extraordinary customer service. Doing it right the first time is essential. As the saying goes, you only have one chance to make the right first impression.

Selecting the right staff is a make or break step in the successful launch of your cosmetic medical center. Do consider using professional help. You can use an agency or consulting company for assistance in finding and interviewing the right professional staff member.

It is paramount that when you decide to become a medical spa, or add aesthetic services to an existing Medical Practice, you need to take a hard look at your staff. I cannot say it enough – customer service is central to success, and your staff can be your best marketing tool – they can make you or break you. Keep this in mind during the interviewing process – you may find yourself looking for different qualities in future hires than you did in past hires.

Both existing and new staff must have the right professional look and convey the desired feeling that matches the atmosphere you want to provide. They must be trained in customer service and understand the principles of pampering.

There can be no compromising on this since the medical spa business is a very service oriented business venture.

Train your staff

Make sure you allow at least two months prior to your opening to hire new staff or give your current staff the additional training they may need. Be sure that the staff has a chance to sample one or more of the services offered by your cosmetic medical spa.

They are your best PR ambassadors, ready and willing to tell anyone who will listen just how extremely amazing your services are and why they can't wait a minute longer to become a client. Then, to keep morale high, do offer your staff one free non-invasive treatment per quarter to perpetuate their eagerness to be your cosmetic medical spa's calling card.

After they receive this "first person" training, you'll be ready to embark on a comprehensive training program. It is not as daunting as it may seem. Most companies that sell products or equipment have trainers that will provide on-site training to your site, or they may provide off-site training. Alternatively, you can hire a professional consultant to provide needed training.

Start with training days as a kind of preview before the public opening.

Then, budget for continued training, which is critical to keep all staff abreast of current and evolving trends. Continuing education is crucial. New and improved equipment using cutting-edge technology is always on the horizon, so training needs to keep apace.

Every few months or so, upgrade your staff's expertise with in-house training, or, better still, send them to a trade show, which not only educates them, but motivates them.

Patient Financing Options

Unlike your medical patients that rely on health care coverage to pay in part or full for their medically oriented appointments, your medical spa service seekers will most likely pay for their services and treatments on a cash basis. While some services and treatments may be relatively low priced offerings, a majority of the services may require a bit of a cash investment. For this reason, just like shopping for a car or a home mortgage, a host of innovative patient financing options has popularized patients' ability to receive aesthetic services without breaking into their savings.

In a recent survey conducted by Inquire Market Research, it was found that 78 percent of patients are more likely to book procedures when a patient financing option is offered.

Patient financing is taking the economic barrier out of the equation through innovative, 12 to 18 month no interest or extended payment plans to comfortably fit the cosmetic procedures into everyone's budget. For example, a $3,000 treatment on an extended 48-month plan, it would cost the patient $79 per month (with a fixed APR.)

Patient financing makes the process simple and affordable, and you would be able to offer multiple procedures and services to the same client.

Ralph Waldo Emerson said it best when he coined this quote: *An ounce of image is worth a pound of performance.*

Before you open your doors to receive your first medical spa client, ask yourself if you can deliver that important ounce of image as well as the pound of performance to create the most sought after medical spa practice in your neighborhood. In fact, if you do all of this correctly, WOMM will spark a revolving door of clientele for your medical spa services.

Remember that all new ventures take time to grow. The beauty of the medical spa business is that in its short history, it has proven to be a quick-return business. It is not unheard of to have a good handle on your success after just six months. However, be prepared to work hard.

If you are a physician, you must be aware that you now have more than a Medical Practice – you have a retail business.

You must change your thinking. You may be staying open longer hours (or different ones) than you would in a normal Medical Practice. The key to success is recognizing the importance of client feedback.

Listen carefully and then continue tailoring your services to meet clients' expressed needs and wants. Make the decision to expand into medical spa services and back up that decision with careful planning and execution.

The rewards will be amazing – both personally and financially.

Section Four: Private Labeling

Opportunities and Pitfalls

Private Labeling involves the creation of new products – or the relabeling of existing products – to be marketed out of a physician's Medical Practice or a medical spa. It represents both opportunities and pitfalls.

It is important to consider that private labeling is valuable when it supports your practice's or spa's overall positioning. The role of private labeling is more than generating revenue, which can be obtained from selling high-end commercially-available precuts, and it's more than an ego trip. It should reinforce what your spa or Medical Practice stands for.

You have your name on the products because you, the practitioner, have (presumably) added value to the products.

Merely putting your name on a product may actually work against you in some situations. For instance, if the customer realizes that it's a product she can obtain elsewhere – usually at a discounted price – she may lose respect for you. And of course, with your name on the label, you'll be held to account for any perceived reactions to the compounded product.

To create a private label product, you need both a product compounding lab to create and manufacture it, and you need a professional product-marketing consultant to help you price it, position it, market it and profit from it.

Here are some critical roles your consultant will play in the process:

- **Selecting a name:** You do not necessarily and automatically want to use the spa's name, or the doctor's name on your private label product. Rather, it may make more of an impact to create a brand name that is "exclusive" to your spa or Medical Practice – in some cases, perceived value may rise. It is hard for someone – a Medical Practice or spa manager or owner – to effectively evaluate this.

116

- **Select a package:** Packaging involves many factors, from box-shape to the choice of labeling vs. silk screening. There are too many factors for amateurs to risk making ill-informed mistakes.

- **Organizing products in groupings:** Products typically come in natural groupings – anti-aging, pigmentation, acne/clear skin, rosacea, etc. Grouping products into focused collections that can be marketed as a group, and that support your spa's or practice's menu – and that are linked to specific patient benefits – are important marketing considerations.

- **Marketing support:** Your branding consultant will help you prepare collateral material – that's marketing jargon for sales brochures and other sales tools – as well as point-of-purchase sales aids. All of these will help to promote your brand, as well as your products and services, effectively. When clients are buying branded products, the marketing support comes from the manufacturer. However, when they are considering private label products, you are the source of the marketing material. There is an advantage to this – your practice's or spa's marketing materials will integrate with the private label's branding message, creating and reinforcing the image you wish to project.

- **Education:** Staff training – to help them both understand and sell the private label products – is essential to success. The staff's motivation (covered elsewhere in the book) will, in this case, be tied to positioning the product collection as a breakthrough, having superior benefits. This will serve as a source of pride to your staff, and will help to guarantee that your staff members support the brand, ensuring financial success.

It's Your Line

Private label products are a natural fit for physicians who want to expand their brands

Branding and marketing are key components to building a successful medical aesthetics practice. An investment in a private label, physician-branded skincare line that carries your logo is a logical extension of your practice's offerings. You can choose the products and ingredients that you feel are most effective. Patients will need to purchase the products directly from your Medical Practice, which helps to build loyalty and provides more opportunities to cross-sell services.

Additionally, private label products can offer a more attractive profit margin than branded lines.

Regardless of the type of product line you choose to private label, the mark-up is entirely up to you, based on your wholesale, development and marketing costs. (For example, your physician-branded eye cream may cost $15 per item from production line to shelf. If you mark it up to $90 and give a 10% commission to your staff, you still net $66). The mark-up on these products can be 300% or more, depending on what the market will support.

Many brand name products that are sold in a physician's office are also available directly through the Internet, or they can be purchased from any other physician carrying the brand. This can result in price wars, a problem avoided by private label products that are only available at your office. There are no price wars, and there is no risk of losing of sales to Internet-based discount retailers.

Types of Private Label

There are three different levels of private label from which to choose. Finding the right fit for your Medical Practice depends on your projected volume, budget and desired level of involvement in the development process.

Basic private label companies offer existing products and lines that can be labeled with your logo. The manufacturer does not alter the formula, but simply places your name and logo onto the packaging. This is the most affordable option, allowing you to launch a physician-branded line for less than $5,000, and can include a full line of products or SKUs.

Custom skincare lines allow you to work with a company's research and development team to tweak existing products by incorporating specific ingredients into the formulations. In addition, you can further customize your products with designer packaging, which costs about $2 and up per jar or bottle. Rates for this option typically start at $10,000 and go up based on the number of products created and the minimum packaging orders required. If you are required to purchase 5,000 jars, keep in mind that they do not need to be filled all at once and they can be labeled for different products.

Proprietary skincare lines ensure that you have unique products and/or ingredients that no other Medical Practice offers. You work directly with a chemist to create your products from scratch. Because this requires testing, proprietary formulation is the most expensive option starting at around $20,000 and increasing based on the number of products you want to create and the type of testing required.

For example, fees can range from $2,500 to $10,000 per product for development and extensive testing.

(NOTE: Co-branding with an established skincare company may be offered to Medical Practices or medspas with distinguished aesthetic services and retail success. This category of physician-branded products would link your name with the company's on the label of every product in the line.)

Choosing the Products

Before embarking on a private label or custom line, you will need to decide upon the number of cosmeceutical products you will carry under your own brand. You may choose to offer one specialty product targeting a specific condition or expand to a full retail line of up to 20 skin and body products.

Reviewing your existing retail sales can help you hone in on products that will be most successful in your Medical Practice. Look at your top-selling retail products as well as back bar products used in your treatment rooms to identify categories that are most popular with your patient base. Also consider the types of products your patients are requesting. Using a questionnaire at check-in can be a valuable way to identify your patients' wants and needs.

Other options to consider include choosing products with highly touted ingredients, such as collagen-stimulating peptides, growth factors, acids or cutting-edge product delivery systems.

Launching just one standalone "Hero" product can start to make you a skincare authority. This is also a good way to get your feet wet, especially if it is a specialty product that can retail in the top end of what your market will bear.

Offering kits or sets of products for specific skin types, such as acneic skin or mature skin, and for follow-up care after skin resurfacing procedures, is another effective way to enter the arena of physician-branded skin care.

Marketing Your Brand

Launching a private label line is a powerful way to build your brand, but it does involve much more than choosing the products and designing a label. You will also be responsible for marketing the new line and training employees on active ingredients and benefits.

With a customized line of products, you become your own skincare company. Skincare manufacturers spend a lot of money each year marketing their brands and training on how to retail said lines.

With private label, your Medical Practice will need to take on many of these duties. Private label and custom skincare manufacturers offer varying levels of support. Most offer graphic designers that can help you create your logo and product labels. Others offer in-office staff training on ingredients and product benefits as well as sales sheets that can be used to create marketing brochures and campaigns.

Following are some of the steps you will need to take to successfully launch a private label line.

- Develop a business and marketing plan, with financial projections to gauge capital and cash flow needs for labeling – hot stamping or silk screening – packaging, marketing and advertising, and the development of collateral materials, such as brochures

- Complete research to identify and procure an effective physician-grade product line

- Come up with a name and logo design for the products

- Create a timeline to determine how long it will take to move from inception to implementation. Generally, you can expect the process to take a minimum of two months. For those opting to create proprietary lines, it can take up to nine months to complete testing, choose packaging, design labels and develop collateral materials.

One way to ease patients into the new line is to offer a mix of well-known branded products and private label products. Branded product lines can help get new clients walking in the door, then get them walking out with your product. This is what happens when a customer goes to Walgreens for an Olay product and walks out with a Walgreen-branded product. It's all about positioning and marketing.

Building Your Brand

Successfully launching a private label line starts with staff training and attractive merchandising. Create a Sephora-like "retail zone" near your reception desk with testers and informative materials. Make your products visually appealing by keeping them clean and fully stocked. Don't be afraid to turn to an expert to give you the goods on how to display your products in an eye-catching way since half the "sell" is in the "seeing." Depending on your budget and taste, your display space can be quite elaborate or tastefully simple. Place small displays of product in every room.

Lucite boxes can be used throughout the Medical Practice to highlight products. This allows patients to start conversations about what types of skincare products they are currently using at home.

Your staff should be capable of discussing all of your product lines with patients. Take advantage of technology today and video your product training to create a sales training library that can be utilized by new hires. And don't forget to send patients home with samples and brochures.

You are in the perfect position to take advantage of the benefits private label has to offer, including increased revenue and a stronger relationship with your patients. Most of whom are more than willing to spend their skincare money with the aesthetic Medical Practice that provides the rest of their cosmetic services.

Private Label Skin Care
Put your name where the money is

It isn't just your profit margin that benefits (from adding a Private Label line). Physicians report that their clients express a new level of trust for their knowledge of the industry, which includes aesthetic treatments as well as home maintenance cosmeceuticals.

The future of Private Label skin care lines in aesthetic Medical Practices is growing not only because savvy owners recognize a burgeoning and lucrative market, but also because they want to offer specialty products that meet the unique needs of men and women seeking cosmetic procedures.

Market research shows that the annual average revenue of a medspa tops $1.5 million. Of that, the annual gross sales account for up to $120,000, 15% of which is accounted for in retail sales. That's significant – but it can be even higher if you offer a Private Line.

Carrying existing retail lines is indeed profitable to your medical spa business, but adding a Private Label offers an even bigger return on investment. And it isn't just your profit margin that benefits. Physicians report that their clients express a new level of trust for their knowledge of the industry, which includes aesthetic treatments as well as home maintenance cosmeceuticals.

Clients can actually enhance the treatments they receive in your offices with your Private Label. They will have the benefit of higher grade, more potent products with a higher percentage of active ingredients than they can find in a drug store or department store. This includes over-the-counter products that are selling for up to $600.

Set the Stage

Whether you choose to begin the process of developing a Private Label on your own or with the assistance of a consultant who specializes in this market, you need to:

- Acquire thorough assessments of the market, competition and demographics

- Develop a business and marketing plan, with financial projections to gauge capital and cash flow needs for labeling (hot stamping or silk screening), packaging, marketing and advertising, and collateral materials, such as brochures

- Complete research, identifying and procuring a physician-grade product line, and naming and trade marking your products

- Review reports on products currently sold in your medspa and used in your treatment rooms to identify categories that are most popular, as well as the types of products your clients are requesting

You will also need to create a timeline to determine how long it will take to move from inception to implementation. Generally, you can expect the process to take about two months. For those opting to create proprietary lines, it can take up to nine months to complete testing, choose packaging, design labels and develop collateral materials.

Recipe for Success

According to case studies, entering the Private Label venue isn't just about profits. Physicians and medspa owners are determined to provide FDA-approved products that perform at the highest level and deliver above and beyond the results their patients expect. They report being more than pleased to have found exactly that. Further, they are impressed by the amount of research, testing and regulated studies that go into developing the products they choose for their Medical Practices.

However, not all Private Label contenders are equal. It is vital to evaluate the vendors in the market, choosing one that not only meets your needs, but also is regulated and performs the necessary testing for FDA-approval. You have three different levels to choose from, depending on your projected volume and budget:

- Basic Private Label companies offer existing lines that allow you to choose from a variety of products that meet your specifications. The manufacturer does not alter the formula, but simply places your name and logo onto the packaging. This is the most affordable Private Label option at under $5,000, and can include a full line of products (approximately 20 stock keeping units, or SKUs).

- The custom line allows you to work with a designer to incorporate specific ingredients into the formulation of, or tweak an existing line. In addition, you may further customize your products with designer packaging, which costs approximately $2 and up per jar or bottle.

  Rates for this option will run from $5,000 and up, depending on the packaging minimum required. If you are required to purchase 5,000 jars, keep in mind that they do not need to be filled all at once and can be labeled for different products.

- The proprietary line ensures that you have unique products that no other medspa can carry. You work directly with a chemist through research and development to create your products from scratch.

  Because this requires testing and FDA-approval, proprietary formulation is the most expensive option, starting around $20,000, depending on the number of products and the amount and type of testing required. For example, fees can range from $2,500 to $10,000 per product for development and testing.

  NOTE: Co-branding with an established skin care company may be offered to medspas with distinguished aesthetic services and retail success. This category of Private Label products would link your name with the company's on the label of every product in the line.

You will need to decide upon the number of products you will carry. You may choose to offer one specialty product targeting a specific condition or expand to full retail line of up to 20 cosmeceuticals. Other options to consider include highly touted ingredients, such as growth factors and antioxidants, or cutting-edge product delivery systems.

Regardless of the type of product line you choose, the mark-up is entirely up to you, based on your wholesale, development and marketing costs.

For example, your Private Label eye cream may cost $15 per item from production line to shelf. If you mark it up to $90 and give a 10% commission to your staff, you still net $66.

The markup on Private Label products can be 300% or more, depending on what the market will support.

Make Private Labeling work for you

Create a "retail zone" near your reception desk with testers and informative materials. Don't be afraid to turn to an expert to give you the goods on how to display your product in an eye-catching way since half the "sell" is in the "seeing." Depending on your budget and taste, your display space can be quite elaborate or tastefully simple.

In addition, your staff should be fully trained to educate patients about the right products for their needs, as well as the proper application and the best regimen to follow. By offering kits or sets for specific skin types, such as acneic skin, and treatment packages for follow-up care after procedures, such as laser treatment or microdermabrasion, your staff need only assess a client's unique needs to finalize the product grouping.

Remember, your products will only be available at your office or through your Web site. Your patients will not be able to purchase your line through any of the discount sites, such as mystore.com or lovelyskinadngreatskin.com. Patient visits to purchase refills give you and your staff the opportunity to promote additional services.

Investing in your name

As an established specialist, your name has become your brand. An investment in Private Labeling is a logical extension of your practice's offerings – and one of the hottest and most obvious revenue sources in the business.

According to the American Academy of Dermatology, at-home skin care products – including Private Labels – are responsible for up to a billion dollars in sales per year.

You are in the perfect position to take advantage of the benefits this industry has to offer, which includes increased revenue and a stronger relationship of trust with your clients.

The bottom line is that most clients are more than willing to spend their skin care money where they get the rest of their cosmetic services.

A Private Label product line and a well-trained, well-informed staff proficient in selling it can add 30 to 40% to your total revenues. So, what are you waiting for?

Resources

Here is a short list of Private Label resources, but the market offers a wide range of choices. Talk to your consultant about the options that best suit your needs.

- Trade shows provide an excellent opportunity to get ideas when you are in the research phase, as well as a resource for the different pieces that go into developing your line.

- MacRAE's Blue Book Industrial Directory of Manufacturers allows you to browse through a wide variety of products that you may need.

Chapter Three: Lights – Camera – Action: Staging and Hosting Events

Events Management
Think "Wedding"

Everybody has experienced a wedding – their own, in most cases, along with the weddings of brothers or sisters, daughters or sons – but even if you've only experienced a "Hollywood Wedding," you've got an idea of what one is like.

And if you can imagine putting together a wedding – a big wedding, with all the bells and whistles – you've know everything you need in order to put together a successful Aesthetics Medical Practice or Spa special event or other business-building project.

The key to success is planning, whether it's for a wedding of for a practice-building event. Except for elopements, visits to the Justice of the Peace, or last-minute spur-of-the-moment "quick, before we sober up" Vegas weddings, all really impressive weddings begin with planning. And planning begins by making a master checklist. With just a few exceptions, the lists are the same.

Wedding	Business Event
1. Wedding Planner & Timetable	1. Event Planner & Timetable
2. Theme	2. Theme
3. Date and Time	3. Date and Time
4. Location or Venue	4. Location or Venue
5. Priest, Preacher or Rabbi	5. Master of Ceremonies
6. Guest List & Invitations	6. Guest List & Invitations
7. Caterer & Flowers	7. Caterer & Flowers
8. Entertainment	8. Entertainment
9. Wedding Favors	9. Gifts and Hand-Outs
10. Rehearsal & Rehearsal Dinner	10. Pre-Event Run-Through

Let's run through those.

Event Planner. Whether this is something you do yourself, something that you assign to your practice manager, or something you hire out, this is essential. Someone has to be in charge. If "everyone's in charge" (i.e., everyone instinctively knows what they're supposed to do) then, in fact, nobody's in charge.

Success happens by accident, not intention. Recommendation: Hire an event planner for a grand opening party – this frees you and your staff up for what you all do best – take care of patients and business. Then, ask the event planner to create a time table for the events – indicating who does what, and when, in order that it all comes together on event day. Your event ambassador should also be able to prepare a briefing book. The briefing book should contain a sales kit, a press kit, before and after photos that relate to the event theme, a sample Q and A session sheet about the topic of the event, third party endorsements (ie, quotes from patients and the technology representative), supportive statistics, reprints of past press appearances).

Theme. This is a central element to the event. Weddings usually have themes – from "back to nature" to "traditional church" – and this defines everything from the location and date/time to the nature of the invitations and the flavor of the edible decorations. So create a theme that focuses on the event – and focuses the event in ways that will bring in business.

Sometimes traditional is best, but sometimes thinking out of the box works. Traditional means having a patient-education component ("this is what botox is and how it works") or announcing a new product, service or facility. Demonstrations of procedures also falls under the realm of traditional, and that can pack the house if you've got an interesting procedure to demonstrate.

Those traditional programs often work – but sometimes, it helps to go beyond traditional, to think out of the box, to make this more than an Amway-like sales pitch.

For example:

Super Bowl Sunday could be a horrible setting for an event – but you could make a Super Bowl Sunday event the hit of the season ... IF you want women who would otherwise be stuck at home, bored beyond tears as they serve up hot wings and cold beers to their significant other and his buddies as they make fools of themselves in some kind of weird annual bonding ritual.

You wouldn't hold an event right before Valentine's Day – unless you're offering free make-overs, in which case it could be standing room only.

"Gal's night out" kind of events can really be effective, especially one that includes free delivery pizza and wings, sent home to the husbands of any woman who actually show up, making it "ok" for them to be away from home at supper time. That may seem a bit pricey, but it could provide a huge pay-off in new clients and new products sold. They'll even come home to a happy and well-fed family.

Think out of the box. Come up with a theme that works for the guests' spouses and families, as well as the guests – and one that also works for building new clients and new business.

Date and Time. You need a date that doesn't conflict with local charitable events, including area hospital events; you need a time that won't require you to close your office for two very long (you will have to shut down if handle this in your own office – but to have it somewhere else means your guests won't see what a great place you have – and that's not a good thing. You also want a date and time that will allow your target audience to turn out in force. Tie your schedule to something that works for you, or find a way to make it work. Most events should not be held during office hours – unless you can come up with a workable exception that makes sense.

Location or Venue. The ideal location in most cases is your office, because it allows you to show off your office. But there could be a case made for having it off-site (at an affiliated spa, for instance) if you make spa treatments part of the program – they're a great draw, but not always possible in a Medical Practice setting. The location should be tied to the theme of the event.

Master of Ceremonies. You don't need a priest, preacher or rabbi to "officiate" the way you do at a wedding, but it often makes good sense to have a third party as your MC – this allows you to more effectively circulate with your guests and not have the pressure of being "on" every instant. The MC can do double-duty if he or she also represents in some way the theme.

If your theme is "get ready for the beach," a well-known local TV weatherman could be a natural – he or she could predict "beach weather real soon" which would tie into getting ready for bikini season. A local workout coach and fitness guru from your strategic ally, the local up-scale gym, could make the same pitch. Almost any time of year would work for the fitness guru, or with a make-over expert from the local Nordstrom's or a major local spa.

Having an MC can be especially important if your event involves you making a presentation to your guests. The MC can hold their attention until you're ready, then introduce you.

Whomever you choose, you want someone who creates confidence, and who is glib on his or her feet.

Even better if he or she adds a little local celebrity buzz to the event. Do not underestimate the importance and impact of local "celebrity," and make use of it in attracting the guests you want – the ones who will become patients or clients.

Guest lists and invitations. These perhaps should be two distinct categories, so let's start with Guest Lists.

a. **Guest List:** Your invitation list should include:

    i. Clients and Former Clients

    ii. Friends of Clients and Former Clients (ask your them to nominate potential guests)

    iii. Prospects – including people you advertise for it

    iv. Civic and community leaders (especially those who might someday become clients)

v. Non-Professional event planners (women who might want to secure your services for "event" make-overs or "event" botoxins – for sororities, wedding parties, pre-25th anniversary events, etc.

b. **Invitations and Promotions:** Your "invitations" should include mailed and emailed invitations that would be professionally designed and written, then mailed or emailed (or both). This is important, and a professional should be called in.

However, the idea of "invitations" should also include other approaches; here again, professionals (PR, Social Networking, Advertising, etc.) should be involved as well.

i. Press releases posted via wire services (BusinessWire, etc.) announcing the event and giving a call-in or social network contact account by which people can RSVP (and give you their contact information). The title of such a press release would be called a PRESS EVENT. Visit Appendix 6 to learn how to draft a press release.

ii. Social networking "invitations" posted on Facebook, Twitter, LinkedIn, etc., and supported by blogs, photo spreads and other "content" that will make people interested in attending

iii. Advertising in local fashion/beauty media, both online and print/broadcast

iv. Posters at strategic allies – beauty salons, spas, fitness centers, department store makeover departments, Fredrick's of Hollywood – any business that shares a common target demographic audience but doesn't compete head-to-head with you for their business

Caterers and Flowers. This means event decorations – there may be catered food (or not) and you might involve flowers (or not) – but whatever you do, you will want to decorate the location – and offering snacks and beverages is almost always an excellent idea. Rely on your professional event planner here – she'll have established business arrangements that should (if you picked the right event planner) get you premium services and discounts.

However, do check to make sure that the events planner isn't getting kickbacks from vendors – that kind of business arrangement does not generate superior quality (vendors providing kick-backs have to cut corners or lose money), and it sure doesn't get you the best prices, since if at all possible, the kick-back will be passed on to the client – you.

Entertainment. In many events, you – the doctor or practice manager – you are the "entertainment," making a presentation about what you do, or about a new procedure or product. But think beyond the box. A soft/light jazz combo could add to the event. The MC might be a budding stand-up comedian who will lighten the event.

On-the-spot makeovers are a form of entertainment, as are character-sketch portrait artists and even palm readers. You can be serious or light, but you want the entire night to be memorable, and great food, great drinks and great entertainment can add to any event.

Gifts and Hand-Outs. This reminds your guests that this is ultimately about business. It might include samples of custom/branded make-up and make-over products you offer, or it might include a "gift bag" with free-service coupons. These coupons should not merely offer discounts, not unless the coupons offer at least a 25% greater discount than the vendors offer on their ads – it's got to be special or it's not worth the paper it's printed on. Include coupons for free services you can offer to your prospects – the goal, ultimately, is to convert guests into paying customers.

Pre-Event Run-Throughs. This is where most events run by physicians or spas falls flat. Practice. No wedding goes forward without a rehearsal, and a rehearsal dinner. That's part of what makes them special, and part of why amateurs (grooms) so seldom mess up on the big day. They rehearsed. Then, and only then, they partied.

Make your event special. Do a run-through the day before, a "dress rehearsal" of the entire event. Make sure everyone on your staff, and every hired gun, is ready. Then reward them by having an event "rehearsal dinner," at a nice place, and pick up the tab. That will put everyone in a confident and positive mind-set when they're ready to move forward.

Bottom line: A wedding is the beginning of the rest of their lives for the participants. It's a big deal, and people who care do the planning, subdivide the responsibilities and make sure everything is done right.

Step-by-Step Guide to Successful Event Planning On Any Budget

Building Your Medical Practice Through Face-To-Face Events

A well run event can bring a significant number of new patients to your aesthetic Medical Practice – or the event can bring together new customers for your proprietary product. However, running an event, whether it attracts 5 or 500 people, can be a daunting task. The skills needed to stage and promote a successful event are far different from the skills needed to effectively treat patients one-on-one – so to prepare for success, check out this guide to successful events.

Before you schedule your event, first stop and think about the purpose of this event. Are you hosting the event to thank your existing patients, or attract new ones? Are you launching a new treatment or product and want to create a buzz among a specific target audience? Or are you just trying to build marketplace awareness of your brand and your Medical Practice?

Identify your goal for the event up front. This will help guide your decisions in planning the event.

Working with your brand and budget, as well as the desired outcome, you should create an experience that your attendees will remember. The event should also positively differentiate your Medical Practice from those of your competition. If you are unsure of where to start, our consultants at beautiful forever offer you our key points as your guide to success:

- **Decide on the purpose of your event**. (education/new procedures, new staff member, patient appreciation, grand re-opening), and make sure that every part of the event – from promotion to hand-outs – reflect that purpose. (see sidebar for our suggestions on calendar of events)

- **Identify a person in your office to take ownership of your event.** This person must be organized and excellent in following up and following through. Designate this person to work with your marketing team.

- **Venue** – how large an event are you planning? Is your office able to accommodate the amount of guests you are expecting? If you are thinking a larger crowd, or perhaps more of a social event, a stylish, upscale hotel or restaurant may be more suitable, you may also consider if space and weather permits, erecting a tent to allow for overflow or to hold the entire event.

- **Sixty days prior to the event**, send a "Save the Date" pre-invitation to put down a marker and get on potential guests' calendars before conflicts arise.

- **Forty-five days prior to the event**, develop a detailed invitation for your event. Paper invitations are more expensive – and more effective. Digital (email, Facebook and Twitter posts, etc.) are less costly, but also less effective. The best solution is often a combination of print/mail and email invitations, each reaching the same individuals to reinforce the message.

- **The invitation should include the date, time and place**, along with a motivating and intriguing topic. It should be created with your "brand identity" and contact information. Always include a "call to action" such as 'Space is limited and many have already secured their place, **so call now!**'

- **Two weeks later**, forward the detailed invitation again with a personalized note. Still have unanswered invites? Call guests and extend a personal invitation.

- **Network your event** and create a version of your invitation to be displayed at your strategically-allied businesses- health clubs, health food stores, salons, etc. Give these strategic allies these flyers, along with additional invitations, 30 days in advance of your event.

  Offer them incentives... bring 3 guests get discounts on products and/or services. You can also consider offering them space at your event. Provided they are not in competition with any of your services have them set up tables and distribute information on topics such as nutrition/diet/wellness.

- **It's often best to encourage response** through your website so that prospective attendees will see the website and learn more about your Medical Practice. You should also be able to add their email addresses to your list, enhancing your database for marketing purposes.

- **Attendance at this event** should be by invitation or pre-registration only. Create an incentive for "bring a friend" (ex. each guest receives five raffle tickets, receive additional five for each friend that that you bring). Please be sure to ask them to preregister.

- **Favorably leverage your relationships with vendors** – get them to underwrite as much of the cost as possible. Encourage vendors to attend and display information or be part of your educational program. (Ex. Allergan, information and specials on Botox and/or Latisse).

  Free samples that are distributed at the seminar are great for prospects who may not come in for treatments but who could still become clients for skin care products.

- **To effectively promote each event**, thirty days in advance of your event, take advantage of free marketing and send out a press release to your entire media contact list and chamber of commerce list. Community service sections of your local cable TV and newspapers are always looking for educational programs for the community.

- **Plan on door prizes**, and be sure to ask vendors to contribute gifts. Gift certificates, gift baskets or a specific highlighted treatment are examples of good door prizes.

- **Most of your guests will anticipate refreshments,** so consider your budget and what type of catering you want. Quality food trays, hors d'oeuvres, water, juice and coffee usually work well.

  You may consider something a bit more upscale with wine and cheese platters, but if you do, be sure to monitor your guests' alcohol consumption.

  Custom desserts beautifully displayed also make a great impression!

- **Be sure to have a designated** person in charge of check in.

- **Upon check out all attendees get a "goodie bag."** Something packaged nicely with samples and information from your product line works well.

- Offer a **'this night only discount'** for attendees who book at the event. It will help them decide that night to come in for treatments. Also offer discounts on products purchased that evening. Be sure to mention you have discounts gift certificates available. Explain finance options so your services are affordable to everybody.

- **If you are holding your event in your office**, schedule patients in the morning so you will have time to prepare and set up. Create a to-do list, the week before and day of.

- **Have soft, mood music playing**. Decorate with fresh flowers. Obviously, the office should be spotless clean. All displays in place and organized. All valuable display items should be put away; don't leave anything to chance.

- **Have staff dressed appropriately.** Depending on location they should be in proper "dinner attire" or if in office, dressed nicely under lab coats, with logo, looks neat and put together.

- **Prep each room with relevant brochures**, as well as before-and-after pictures – your own (preferably) or company stock photos. Keep displays of product.

- **Patient flow should be directed by a concierge** or greeter (with name tag)- you can use your practice manager – having patients go from room to room seeing each procedure, then given the chance to hear about it and ask questions, enhances their experiences.

- **The area within the office** where staffs are taking money for products, gift-certificates, etc., should have a price list available for all the procedures with special prices being offered that night and discounts on gift certificates.

- **To handle visitor flow**, depending on the amount of people attending ... (40-60 makes sense) you will need two people taking money and giving clients instructions and two people making appointments.

- **Doctor and key staff** should be available to speak with guests ... explanation of services, answering questions etc.

Advertising and Promotion

Start with internal marketing – with signage, and "working" your database – this is your least expensive and most effective form of event marketing.

Do you need to advertise your event? This may depend on the goal of the event and the intended audience. If so, create an advertising budget and goals. You should identify advertising methods – email and the web, TV and radio, magazines and newspapers.

The correct medium for you will depend on the type of guests you're trying to recruit. Consider using new social media tools and events websites, especially geo-targeted ones, to promote your event.

Examples include LinkedIn, Facebook, and Twitter. Make sure to design and distribute your ads, emails or letters with ample time to receive responses.

> *We have found that in our market, a mix of media seems to work most effectively. Each of our socials has a different theme, with a different audience, and a variety of advertising has proved to be the best way of reaching our target audiences.*

Follow Up on Each Event

Now that you have created an amazing event and provided everyone with a memorable experience ... what next? Follow up! This can be a simple strategy if someone is in place to follow up. If you need help beautiful forever will design a follow up system for you that will make your facility even more unforgettable.

Start at the beginning by creating an attendee list which requires complete contact information: name, address, phone and e-mail. Add this new information to your existing software-based database, and be sure to include in the information, the event they attended.

The next step should involve sending a follow up note telling each visitor how great it was to meet them – then invite each of them to call with any questions. Add another event date or a reminder of an event incentive that is still available or attach a card with a discount on their next service.

Be sure to include your list of attendees as part of your e-mail blasts and direct mail campaigns, (ex. My Emma, Constant Contact, Vertical Response are good examples). Create groups for future events on different topics.

Don't forget to follow up for people that didn't show...they should be called right after your event and offered something such as a free consultation to get them to come through your door.

We hoped to reach out to the community and re-introduce ourselves with the re-Grand Opening. I believe we accomplished that and much more! We acquired new patients and expanded the breadth of purchases of our existing clients. It was a great event; we are still booking appointments from it even two weeks after the celebration.

Conclusion

With proper planning and implementation your events will always reflect your image, provide you with valuable exposure to new prospective patients and will provide attendees with a very memorable experience that has people talking and anticipating your next event.

Continually build your brand and create a buzz in your local market! Beautiful forever consultants can assess your brand and marketing material... contact us for a complimentary assessment.

Check the Appendix for event planning tools.

Chapter Four: The Write Stuff

Written communications remains at the heart of marketing and promotion for Medical Practices and medi-spas.

This begins with branding the message – part of the overall branding process, but critical to include in each message – then involves public and media relations, printed (including Internet) advertising, social networking in all its myriad ways, as well as books and eBooks.

No doctor should be without a book that he or she has "written," one that positions the Medical Practice or spa to potential clients in a positive and impressive fashion.

Section One: Branding and Communicating Your Message

Properly managed, a practice's brand is typically its most valuable asset. A compelling brand can create patient loyalty and preferences strong enough to overcome intense competition and price differences.

Branding is a technique that all businesses and individuals can use to effectively market themselves and their services. Your personal brand consists of your ultimate vision or mission, the products and services you're offering and how you communicate all of these elements to your target audience.

Personal branding is very powerful because it sends a clear, consistent message about who you are and what you have to offer. A strong, authentic personal brand helps you become known for what you're good at, sets you apart from everyone else, and can position you as a niche expert.

One of the quickest ways to jump start your personal brand is to identify your highest value touchstone. What is the one thing that you can be known for that you excel at?

Your touchstone must be something that you constantly and faithfully over deliver. This is the key to gaining patients and giving it that recurrent push. It must also be something that is easily identifiable. Clear, concise, and recognizable is what you are going for.

You should begin by defining your objective. Determine what you are trying to accomplish, who you are and who your target market is. Define your best prospect and get into their wants and needs.

Next, define your message. Your messaging must be authentic. It must speak directly to the heart of your target market. Keep in mind that your prospective patient doesn't typically want what you are selling they want the result of what you are selling.

Remember that your brand is a promise of quality and value and a commitment to provide consistent performance and a reliable level of service. Patients value and pay more for that level of service because they can place their trust in the brand.

You must be able to deliver what your brand idea says you are going to deliver.

There are an overwhelming number of tools at your disposal to begin to brand yourself. One thing to keep in mind when choosing tools is to ask yourself if this is where you target market can be found. Does your prospective patient interact in this network or with this tool? Find the right places that get right to the heart of the market you are targeting.

Now that you have defined your objective, messaging and tools, it is time to implement.

Reflect your brand in everything you do, including your personal network, your use of technology, office staff and surroundings, your appearance, your volunteer activities, etc.

You must ensure the brand consistently delivers on its unique promises and that the brand messaging is clear, consistent, and compelling. The brand character must be defined and socialized to everyone in your office so they can support, sell and market the product in a manner consistent with the essence of your brand. Inconsistent branding and messaging destroys the most important aspect of a brand – delivering a promise of value that patients can trust.

Only by focusing on, and delivering, your brand messaging in a consistent manner will you be able to build a positive and lasting impression in the mind of your patients. All visual and verbal brand identity must be "On Brand". Each time your brand delivers a compelling message that is "On Brand", it earns trust.

Here are some tips to stay "On Brand:"

- Develop a great logo – display it everywhere

- Put your key brand messages in writing – every staff member should be aware of your brand attributes

- Make sure that everything you do communicates your brand message (your website, what your staff wears, how they answer the phone, your sales and advertising materials, promotions and special offers, etc.)

- Develop a tagline – a concise statement that captures the essence of your brand

- Create brand standards for your website, logo, your print or e-mail materials (use the same color scheme, look and feel)

- Deliver on your brand promise. Once you develop your key messages and benefits – make sure you're consistent in every interaction with your patients

First Impressions

From the domain name, template, design, and images that you use, people instinctively scrutinize these points to identify if the site would satisfy what they're looking for. With just one look at your brand through your blog or website, people immediately get a feel of what you have to offer.

For example, when visitors arrive at your web site, let them know immediately what you do and why they should care.

View your site through the eyes of a new visitor. It should spell out exactly what your brand stands for and influence your patients that you are relevant and the best choice and not to think of you as just another option. . If this not the case, redesign it so your message and identity are unmistakable.

Blogs and Social Media

Addressed in greater depth in the next section of the book, blogs and social networking play a critical role in business building. Building your brand using blogs and social media allows you to develop new (and strengthen existing) relationships, which often leads to everything from brand awareness, loyalty and word-of-mouth marketing.

Consider using popular, free options like blogs, Twitter, Facebook, LinkedIn, YouTube, and so on. For smaller-businesses without the manpower to efficiently manage too many destinations, you should consider testing each of these to determine which sites will work best for you. This will become your central destination. All your other online destinations should link back to specific relevant locations on your website.

The goal is to publish useful information that people will want to talk about -- and then share with their own audiences. This creates additional ways for people to find your branded destinations and it can lead to higher rankings from search engines like Google.

Determine where your target audience already spends their time. That is where you should spend your time also. Engage in the conversations happening there.

You can also retain expert beauty bloggers to help promote a product, create a unique event, or in other way turn their hoard of followers into useful and valuable prospects.

Join relevant online forums and/or blogs, and write posts, publish comments and answer questions. By offering useful information you can start leading them to your own branded destinations – particularly your core branded online destination.

Success in blogging and social media marketing depends on being useful and developing relationships. If you spend all of your time promoting then no one will want to listen to you.

A good rule for your social media marketing efforts is to spend a small percentage of your time in self-promotional activities and conversations, and the majority of your time on non-self-promotional activities. In time, you'll see your business grow from your efforts.

Section Two: Public and Media Relations

Public Relations and Lead Generation

Public relations – working with the news media to receive free and favorable coverage in newspapers, on TV, on the Radio or on an Internet News site – can and should be part of an effective lead-generation business-building program that brings qualified potential patients into a company's sphere of influence – leading, ultimately, to direct negotiations and closed business deals. PR cannot close – but, with proper handling, PR can lay the groundwork for effective closing of important business contracts and sales.

First, you must understand the difference between marketing and PR. Marketing is also known as propaganda. Advertisements fall into the category of marketing. Advertisements work well when promoted through a multi prong strategy that involves repeat advertising. Repeat reminders of what an individual has already determined to be valuable based on third party endorsements are required to secure results from advertising. Third party endorsements may come in the form of word of mouth referrals; a before and after photo book; social media likes and shares from friends; and the like. PR is another form of third-party endorsements. Public relations is founded on facts; not propaganda. Public relations can be just as powerful as a word of mouth referral when a credible media outlet selects your story for publishing in print or airing on T.V.

The newspaper is the medium that provides the most in-depth information. Newspapers expand on the short stories presented on TV and Radio. They allow for more complete reporting. Furthermore, newspapers are easily accessible, reaching wide audiences. Local or regional publication exposure can have a ripple effect by receiving the endorsement of national press. Print media can be effective patient acquisition tool or used as a testimonial of your practice's services. The right broadcast press can produce remarkable results in patient acquisition. The main criteria for a newscast are the inevitable consideration: "Is the event newsworthy?" Because most news broadcasts tend to focus on "unhappy" events such as the war, stations are often looking for a positive story to equalize negative segments. Human-interest segments such as a patient story that includes a fully accredited doctor can fulfill this void.

A strong public relations presence can provide many benefits. Public relations can be a beneficial patient acquisition tool and help increase patient satisfaction levels by providing critical information so that patients are equipped to make better educated decisions. Public relations may also help to plan the future destination of the spokesperson's (the doctor) career. Many news stories are viewed by policy makers and organization leaders. Published stories may broaden career options in final years, should the spokesperson choose to turn to education, focus in a specific specialty area, or decide to participate in other opportunities as a key opinion leader. Weather a practice decides to conduct in-house public relations or out-source public relations, a public relations presence is an essential component of any medical practice today in elective medicine.

Challenges Associated with the Press

Working with reporters can be difficult at best. As reporters field through the burgeoning number of press inquiries each day, it is easy for your practice to get caught behind other press inquiries fighting for visibility. Often times, there is a low probability of a media person finding your story. A strong public relations management solution helps to bridge this information gap. The following two fundamentals are important to understand when conducting any public relations campaign that involves the press.

Press Needs and Deadlines

First and foremost, it is important to understand that the media chooses what is considered news and how the news ultimately appears in the press- not a public relations representative or spokesperson. Knowing the ideology behind news including, how reporters establish what is newsworthy, is important in order to receive the right exposure for your practice. Equally important, there is no guarantee that public relations efforts will result in aired or printed press. However, the contribution of your practice's good will through public relations can be very appealing for your practice in the long term.

The Journalist Perspective

Journalists all have the same goal- to get a story in a short time frame. <u>Deadlines are extremely important to the press</u>. If you fall short of the media's deadline, the story will be created without your contribution. Secondly, prepared materials such as Doctor Biography (short paragraph noting credentials and topics you can comment on), scripts, before and after photos, patient testimonials (in the form of video or written quotes), and statistics are very appealing to reporters. These tools help reporters quickly establish credibility to support your point of view. In fact, knowing how the press likes to receive information (in the forms press releases, press kits, video news releases, letters to the editor, opinion editorial articles and letters of endorsement) is very important for a successful campaign. Finally, disregarding an editor's deadline can risk the relationship between your office and the media should they contact your office with a question about a specific medical topic.

The Spokesperson Perspective

Whether you choose to outsource public relations or conduct public relations in-house, a staff member or public relations firm has to be selected who can be available anytime to answer questions from the media, monitor the progress and manage the public relations results. Often times, a medical practice has a dedicated staff member that can act as a liaison for the media and/or an external public relations firm. The key spokesperson for the press in medicine will typically be a doctor who is skilled and ready to meet the press with prepared standard responses to all possible press inquiries. Strong communication is key when it comes to public relations in medicine. Reporters cannot be authorities in every subject matter. Since they operate on tight deadlines, they need to quickly and efficiently pool resources to validate their facts before writing a story. In these cases, they usually contact a public relations firm to locate one or more "experts" (authorities) in the specific field that they are reporting on. If they have an established relationship with a reliable source for information, such as a PR representative or internal staff member at your practice, they may also contact the experts (authorities) directly. In fact, in order to produce a story, reporters will typically require interviews with at least two or more credible individuals in order to complete a story. A media source is a person who is skilled and knowledgeable in a certain field of specialty- an authority or expert. Whenever reporters are covering stories that deal with a particular topic, they will contact an appropriate media source(s) to confirm the knowledge that the reporter has acquired, ask advice and request other relevant information. Reporters in medicine find media sources very helpful. With the large number of medical procedures available, new technology, and forward thinking legislation, it is very difficult for reporters to do their job without the help of medical media sources, specifically those who have substantiated themselves as credible sources of information on specific subject matters. Establish yourself as an expert that leads the press to you as the go to person.

More than ever before, medical practices today have the opportunity to become media sources for the press. And while media needs require the ability to reach credible doctors for information (as media sources), doctors cannot manage public relations without the assistance of the right hand- able to meet press requirements with great internal coordination. Most importantly, appearances in the press lend credibility to your practice, helping to get your name, mission and philosophy in front of public audiences.

Selecting The Right Staff

Working with print and broadcast media means knowing how each company works. Press relations are personal relationships with media representatives. Meetings between yourself and media representatives can be informal as you discuss healthcare issues of mutual interest or new innovations. It is more important for the carrier of the message and the message itself to come from a credible party when compared to a person with a sales or marketing background who knows how to craft and deliver marketing messages. In essence, the qualities of the right PR staff person are much different than the person who handles advertising. This individual must complete the following tasks to support successful PR missions, as follows.

Selecting the Contacts: Newspapers, Local Bloggers, Radio and TV

For starters, you will want to select media outlets that align with your mission, such as health bloggers or health magazines. Certain community outlets can also be valuable since you are connected to your local area. To do so, review the editorial calendars for the upcoming year to identify those that would be most receptive to your message.

- Determine which stories would be appropriate to reach your target audience, including any special features or issues.

- Exam guidelines and deadlines.

- Include all gathered information in a Contact List.

The Contact List

It's also important to know the roles in print and broadcast media. Title and responsibilities of staff members at outlets vary. Generally, the Managing Editor is responsible for the overall performance and nature of the publication or broadcasting company. The Editor generally assigns specific assignments to reporters for news stories. The Reporter is responsible for collecting all necessary material, including the completion of interviews and preparation of stories. Certain editors will accept your story ideas (in the form of a press release) and submit them to the Editor or direct you to other personnel that might be interested in your point of view. Yet, you must be prepared to deliver all necessary information to the outlet before sending your message off. Your contact list should include the following.

- Names, Addresses, Phone Numbers, Faxes, Email Addresses.

- Publications' and broadcasting company deadline times and dates, format requirements, story preferences and all other pertinent information. It is also important to note that every reporter, editor and media outlet has their own preference for receiving materials. It is important to understand the reporters and editors requirements: regular mail, fax, email, or hand delivery.

- Category including, Trade, Newspaper- Weekly & Daily, Wire News Services, Columnists, Radio and Television.

Making Contact

The communication begins with a phone call, fax, email or us mail (depending upon the reporter's preference) that discloses the message (press release information) that you wish to communicate. This press release or press kit includes patient testimonials (in the form of quotes within the press release), before and after photos, third party support (i.e. letters of endorsement) and possibly reprints of relevant press. The information may include a letter to the editor, opinion editorial article or a video news release as well.

- Create a Sample Q and A Script: Interviews with the press can be taxing without a prepared script. A well-prepared script also helps to ensure that an accurate message will appear and not be cut by the publication or broadcasting company editing department. Pre-recorded tapes may run from 10 to 60 seconds, containing 25 words for 10 seconds and 140 words for 60 seconds. Publications and/or broadcasting companies may print or have an announcer read a well-edited press release, providing that the press release contains the critical components to make it newsworthy.

- Prepare a Briefing Book: The preparation of a briefing book that provides the speaker with key information offers the potential to improve communication and streamline the message for the audience. The briefing book typically includes information about the topic, relevant and supporting statistics, background information, and key messages that the physician wishes to communicate about the topic. The briefing book should also include sample questions to expect during the interview, as well as, answers to such questions. Special contact info such as a special website for PR campaigns and a special phone number is helpful to have to track results from campaigns. This information and the sample Q and A may also be given to the reporter to help them keep on track with the message. Other pertinent components to a briefing book would include the location, time and date of the interview. A notepad and recorder are also recommended.

- Seek Out Resources for Assistance: In-house time requirements can be reduced and the results may be optimized with the aid of a professional PR representative.

The Materials

Public relations campaigns require in-house coordination weather an external firm is assisting or not. In order to present information to the press, it is important to be prepared with the following materials.

- Before and After Photos: For any press relating to an aesthetic medical procedure, standard before and after photos is important.

- Patient Testimonials: Patients testimonials in the form of quotes are crucial for consumer stories relating to elective medical procedures.

- Hold Harmless Agreement: Patients must sign a photo release and hold harmless agreement in order to use the quotes or pictures in any form of non-confidential exposure.

- About the Doctor Biography: A short biography denoting credentials, training, education, membership affiliation and practice focus (outlining specific areas that the doctor is qualified to comment on) is important to have on hand for press reference.

- Third Party Support: Securing the support of an Industry Analyst or Leader (in the form of a quote or letter of endorsement that supports the practice's position), a pharmaceutical representative or equipment representative quotes, patient quote, and/or statistics demonstrating the problem and solution that you are commenting on, all go a long way in receiving the support of a publication or broadcasting company.

- Information Forms: Press likes to receive information in a specific format. Formats for materials include press releases, press kits, letters to the editor, opinion editorial articles and letters of endorsement, and video news releases.

- Reprints: Reprints of published articles that relate to your specialty can be beneficial to include in press submissions.

Know the Components

There are three components that are crucial to successful PR campaigns. The first involves becoming a Media Source, a practice that lets the press know every time something newsworthy occurs in the practice on an ongoing basis. This is accomplished in the form on ongoing press releases approximately once a month in the right format- component two. The third component involves what you do with a clip – to effectively and comprehensively leverage its impact AFTER you get it – that counts.

Becoming a Media Source with Your Press Releases

The content in your press releases plays a role in how you message is perceived by the media outlets. Your content should be a short, one page synopsis that paints a picture of your story. Since reporters are usually working on deadlines, they must be able to swiftly denote the WHO, WHAT, WHERE, WHEN, and WHY of your information in the first sentence.

See Appendix Six for a sample Press Release.

Press Release Distribution

Decide who should receive your press release- all media outlets or one. While sending your release to many media outlets increases your chances that one of them will pick up your story, a specific and exclusive story that is published by a specific reporter has a much better chance of going to print or airing. Most media staff members think twice before disregarding a story that is an exclusive. There are two opportunities for follow up after a story prints, including:

A) *After a story that you submitted appears:* call the reporter or send a personal thank-you note to not only thank them, but inform them about the results that the story produced. Examples include--- new patients, interest in other procedures (which may prompt another story).

B) *After a story that relates to your specialty appears:* If you have a comment, different angle, and/or a different media channel to contact about a story that was produced by a specific media channel, let reporters know about your point of view in the form of an second press release. A perfect time to have your story angle appear is when the press corps are airing or printing other relevant stories.

Other PR Forms: Video Marketing, Letter to the Editor, Opinion Editorial Article and Press Kits

Three formal means for capturing the attention of an editor and reaching a targeted audience about your angle are through video marketing, a letter to the editor, an opinion editorial article or a press kit.

Lights Camera Action! You're Not Finished Yet! Video Marketing Is In

So...you're the proud new owner of expensive equipment. Congratulations! It's now time to capture the external market. You may choose to create a video about your practice's mission. You may opt to tape an event you have planned. You may select to make video testimonials of your happy patients. You may also elect to make educational videos about procedures or how to information that is motivating and useful to consumers.

Once you select your best video, your web company needs to highlight your winning video on your website-front and center. You'll want to create a You Tube channel and post all of your videos there. You'll also want to link your You Tube from your website and vice versa. Then, you have to find a way to tell potential patients that you're the best person to do their procedure. How? Through video marketing! Video marketing is the modern way to share your story via your website, social media and in your own words (or those of your fantastic success story patients).

Don't believe me? Here are some staggering statistics about video marketing:

- 38.2 billion videos were viewed online in the second quarter of 2014. That's a massive 43% increase over the same quarter last year. (Adobe)

- YouTube reaches more US adults ages 18-34 than any cable network. (Nielsen)

- Videos increase people's understanding of your services by 74%. (Digital Sherpa)

- It's 50x easier to achieve a Page 1 ranking on Google with a video. (Forrester Research)

- On average, a website visitor will stay two minutes longer on a site when they watch a video. (Comscore)

According to the number counters at YouTube, 100 million Internet users watch video online every day. Of course, some people are tuning into watch a viral video of a goofy dog...but many others are looking for advice on how to do something or how to make something work better. Many of them are looking to buy a service or product to improve themselves. This means a success story about a fantastic new procedure is the perfect way to sell you and your services, without directly selling. You're selling success and the promise of a youthful result.

So why do you...an accomplished physician/business owner need to embrace video? It's because people are visual learners. Sadly, they don't read. You need to get in there, introduce yourself...and once they love you...show them why you're better and the right person to perform their procedure.

Video allows you to clarify your key points of differentiation from your competition. In a crowded cosmetic field, that's vital. With a well-structured, targeted video marketing plan, you can:

- Build a personal connection with potential patients before the consultation

- Enhance credibility, trustworthiness, likeability

- Build web traffic

As with all good things, there's a cost. Professional video is worth the investment, but it is just that, an investment. Anytime you or your work is captured on video, and presented to the public, you want to put your best face forward. You can certainly produce a web video using your iPhone, iPad or other device, but it will not be as professional that patients have come to expect from you and your practice. Thus, hire a professional crew

158

accordingly. Look for one that has extensive experience in medical video production for the web and the experience to coach you to bring out your best. These experts will also be able to advise you where you post your video for optimum performance (your website, social media, etc). They can work in concert with your web team to make sure you get the biggest "bang for your marketing buck."

And believe me, potential patients know the difference between good and bad video (just as they know the difference between good and bad cosmetic results). Professional polish on a video, with an appropriate budget, is often the best way to go. The costs will easily be covered by booked procedures. As the saying goes, "you get what you pay for."

Bottom line, if you're not using video marketing, you're missing out on a huge opportunity to sell your points of differentiation in this competitive cosmetic market. The video sells you, before the first call or consultation.

We offer coaching and scripting. You can send us your home video and we can polish it up for you. Learn key facts before you post a video. Once it's posted on the Internet, there is no editing it.

Letters to the Editor

One of the most read sections in publications is the Letters to the Editor column. Consequently, a letter to the editor makes is an advantageous location to have your message printed. This section of the newspaper is devoted to discussing opinions about current social issues and events.

When a relevant article appears about your specialty that you feel you can comment on, write a letter to the editor. This letter may either endorse the printed point of view or dispute it, whichever is appropriate. The following factors are important when considering a letter to the editor.

Special Considerations: Letters to the Editor

• Check and double-check any facts you refer to in your letter. Be as accurate and fair as possible.

• Be brief. Edit, edit, edit.

• Pay Attention to the Readers. Consider that hundreds will read the finished letter.

• Be timely. Your Letter to the Editor must be received within one week after a related story appears.

• Letters to the Editor are about your point of view. Make only a small reference to your practice. The information in a comprehensive CV about the doctor is all that is required to provide reference to the author or the practice.

• Sign the Letter to the Editor. Letters to the Editor must be signed.

Opinion Editorial Articles

Op-ed is the short term for an opinion editorial article. There are publications that like receiving a well-written, well-edited article from an independent credible individual. The op-ed article provides a perfect opportunity to present your practice's ideas, objectives and goals. After the op-ed is published, reprints can be used for mailings to patients, referring doctors and specialty related key organization members.

Op-eds are an excellent means for raising the public awareness about all medical news. They also have the potential to educate policy makers.

Op-Ed Tips

•   Exclusivity: Always send an op-ed article to one newspaper.

- Spacing and Margins: Most newspapers like op-eds to be 750- 800 words, double-spaced with wide margins. The Sunday edition may have different spacing and margin requirements.

- Easy to Read: First, op-eds should state what the problem is. Second, the article should show how your idea will or has solved the problem. Finally, the focus should be of general appeal to the audience.

- Timing is Everything: Op-eds should be timely, talk about today's problems/solutions, not last week's.

- Pay Attention to the Readers: Consider that at least hundreds will read the finished op-ed article.

- Edit, edit edit.

- Submission: Direct your article to the Editorial Editor or the Op-Ed Page Editor. Use the person's name and title, spelled correctly.

Building Your Press Kit

Press kits are valuable to build on. A press kit should include the About the Doctor Biography, at least three upcoming press releases, reprints of past press appearances, letters of endorsement (ie. patient testimonials, third party endorsements from industry analyst and technology representative, sample Q and A's that accompany press releases. An information sheet about how your practice works can also set your practice apart from the competition. The press kit may be made available in your office waiting room and during events. The press kit may be used to mail to press contacts when established as a full kit to solicit more press appearances and/or medical advisory board capacity in the media outlet.

Maximizing Your Impact

A Letter to the Editor, Op Ed Article, Press Kit, Video or Press Kit may be a follow up to a press release. Here are some things that can and should be done to maximize the impact of each PR success:

Put each favorable press appearance – as soon as it comes out – on your website press room.

- Do NOT link to them – the media often "retires" articles after a period of time, whereas their use to you is timeless.

- Best bet: use a screen-capture.

- Second-best: post with the media's logo 𝕿𝖍𝖊 𝕹𝖊𝖜 𝖄𝖔𝖗𝖐 𝕿𝖎𝖒𝖊𝖘 WALL STREET JOURNAL graphic to show where it came from.

Send out each press appearance screen capture, via email (with an appropriate cover note and a link back to your website so they can see the press appearance).

Send to:

- All of your patients, for referral-development purposes.

- To all of your referral sources and "influencers."

- To all of your hot prospects.

- To all of your longer-term prospects.

- Through your PR firm or inside counsel, to media (reporters, editors, producers, bookers) who cover you or your market space – with an appropriate note that makes the press appearance a validator, rather than something that has "used up" the media's interest.

Priority mail copies to internal (sales), referring physician and external (prospects, patients who need reinforcement or who could become referral sources).

- Send them hard-copy clips (reprints, available from most media outlets, usually at reasonable prices) along with appropriate, personal (and personally-signed) letters

- Or, less formally, send it with post-it notes and brief hand-written messages attached to the press appearance.

Put the press appearances in the media kit or press kit – the virtual kit online and any hand-out kits you may have.

- a. If the kit is electronic, provide a link to the press appearance screen capture.

- b. If the kit is printed, include a reprint of the press appearance with other sales-promotion and sales-support materials.

Quote from the press appearances in future sales tools and press releases.

Once sufficient press releases are in hand, create a sales tool (a brochure, for instance, or a web page) that is little more than a string of linked-together quotes from press appearances, all singing your praises.

There are other, specific uses that can be made of effective press appearances in specific instances – for instance, trade shows permit press appearances to be turned into creative hand-outs (printed on coffee mugs, for instance, or in some other way made permanent). These solutions here are "generic" and universal in their application – anybody can (and everybody should) use them.

Section Three: Internet Marketing

Using Internet Marketing to Build Business

If you want to be successful in the real world, it helps to be successful in the virtual world of blogging and social networking. This requires both 'content' and 'conversation' – and while the latter should come naturally, 'content' is something you have to work at.

We recommend building layer on layer with the same information, repackaged for different people. Some like to read. Some like to view. Some like formal and scholarly. Some like more casual and conversational. You can give everybody what they want with the same information. Here's how.

Develop a list of related topics which could be chapters in a book – the eBook you're going to write.

Then, for each topic, write a series of blogs – conversational discussions of the topic – around 750 words each. Then discuss the same information on a video camera and post them as video blogs on YouTube.

Then, in a more formal and scholarly way, write the material from several blogs into a white paper or case study that covers the topics in more depth.

Finally, weave the blogs and white papers into chapters, pull them together, and you've got an eBook. Now, you're an author. And an expert!

beautiful forever ghost writers can make the process painless with a simple phone interview

How to create valuable content for your website.

Building on Blogs

Creating Valuable Web Content

There is a simple three-step process for developing outstanding and compelling content for your website by using short blogs to build longer content around compelling topics.

A good blog can run from 250 to 300 words – some are longer, but they don't need to be. However, useful and topical web content often runs longer than 250 words, so, what do you do? We have developed a simple means of creating useful web content by writing short, topical blogs that are planned, in advance, to be the building-blocks for longer content. Here's what you do …

First, there are a few forms of content that tend to be appealing for blog readers, including:

1. Business and Financial Stories: Focusing on the cosmetic medical outlook or strategy, key opinion leaders, new practices and/or doctors.

2. Consumer Human Interest Stories: Focus on stories of human interest such as a happy patient who made a significant improvement in their appearance because of their doctor and choice in technologies. This may include quotes from the doctor, one or more patients and perhaps, another third party (such as a technology spokesperson).

3. Specialty Specific Stories: Focusing on relevant trade, specialty, or new products and technology such as a technology device - being the first FDA approved.

4. How To Stories: Focusing on how to solve a problem, such as an interest in cosmetic surgery.

Blog Format

Use short active words. The complete story should not be more than 300 words. The tone may be lighthearted or highly educational in nature. Attach an image. Viewers of blog content tend to remain interested when an image is attached. Write blogs one month in advance and prepare four blogs at a time. Upload one blog each week onto your website. Link each story on the social media websites, such as, Facebook and LinkedIn. By linking your blog stories, you may have the opportunity for search engine optimization results after consumers from these social networking sites engage by clicking on the link. The words in the title of the story should be the key words you want to drive traffic from. You should also use these key words in the beginning of the first sentence and as you scan through the paragraph left to right. Speak to your web developer about the key words you want traffic from. Generally speaking, key words or phrases are the words that people are likely select to type into their Internet browser when conducting a search on a search engine.

Come up with an important topic, such as "How do I decide if cosmetic surgery is right for me?" (This is just a hypothetical topic, used for illustration purposes. Then, take this broad topic and, creating an outline, break it down into major sub-topics and minor sub-topics, like this:

How do I decide if cosmetic surgery is right for me?

o   Do I feel less than happy about my current appearance?

o   To achieve the self-image enhancement I'm looking for, could simple and safe image-enhancing cosmetic surgery be part of the solution?

o   Can I see myself having this surgery – does it fit into my self-image, or the self-image I'd like to have?

Next, you take these rather broad topics and break them down into smaller sub-topics, such as this example:

How do I decide if cosmetic surgery is right for me?

o   Do I feel less than happy about my current appearance?

- Is my unhappiness about something specific in my appearance (a facial feature, for instance)?

- Or is my unhappiness more general, relating to my overall appearance?

- Is this unhappiness something that can be addressed by simple and safe cosmetic surgery (a facial feature, for instance)?

- Or is my unhappiness inherent in who I am (height, weight, skin coloring, etc.)?

o To achieve the self-image enhancement I'm looking for, could simple and safe image-enhancing cosmetic surgery be part of the solution?

- Would I need a single procedure?

- Or would I need a series of smaller building-blocks procedures?

o Can I see myself having this surgery – does it fit into my self-image, or the self-image I'd like to have?

- Can I afford the simple and safe cosmetic surgery that would help me change that appearance feature?

- Will those closest to me support me in my decision to have a simple and safe image-enhancing cosmetic surgery procedure?

Remember, this outline is just a "for-example" illustration, and not the outline you should use in reaching your patients. You'll want to pick subjects that will both address concerns of patients and prospects, but they should also be subjects that will help you to attract prospects and keep patients' loyalty.

Each of these sub-topics can be addressed in a relatively short blog, each of which will find a receptive audience. Then, when they're all completed, they can be strung together, following the outline, into a longer document that is also useful.

A major goal of blog writing should be a casual, conversational style – imagine you are talking to one individual who trusts and respects you, who has a real question (the subject of the blog) and is looking to you for a clear, understandable answer.

There are several ways of writing these kinds of personal, casual-style blogs, all of which work, even (or perhaps especially) for those who are not particularly comfortable with writing.

In one workable approach, you can sit in a room with a tape recorder or video recorder and have someone "play the role" of the patient and actually ask you the question you've identified for the blog topic. Then you answer this person, just as you would answer a patient or prospect. Have your answer typed up, edit it for style and content, and you have a blog.

Alternatively, you can retain a professional ghost-writer, a PR professional who is skilled in writing consumer-oriented content. This pro will ask you the questions – in person, by phone or via Skype, and take notes on your answers, then write them up in a clear, concise conversational style.

Once you have your short blogs written, post them in the blog-section of your website, or have your webmaster create for you a blog-site that is linked to your website (there are advantages to both approaches, and – in fact – you can maximize your impact by using both approaches).

Then, when all of them on a given subject are completed, you can pull them together (or have your ghost-writer pull them together) into a single, integrated document, which can be published on your website, distributed via PDF or even published in brochure format.

The key is simple: get the most use out of each piece of writing, reaching the widest number of members of your target audience.

There is another use for this material, one that is often overlooked. Next to Google, YouTube is the most widely used search engine.

You can capitalize on this by creating video blogs on each of the sub-topics you've written (above), then create yet another video – what is known as a "white board" presentation, and discuss the entire topic covered in the series of video blogs.

When you create a video blog, Hollywood-like slick production values are actually a negative – people want to see something that's more "real." Sit in front of an uncluttered professional background, such as a bookcase, and speak to the key points covered in each blog.

Do not read from a script – use bullet-points to keep you on target, but speak from the heart. It might help to have someone right off camera to whom you are talking – this keeps it personal.

Video blogs can run from 90 seconds to 3-5 minutes, but not longer. If it runs longer, break it up.

That's all there is to it.

In-Depth Social Networking For Professional Medical Practices

Building Your Business or Professional Medical Practice through Effective Social Networking

Introduction – The Way It's Always Been …

Having worked with private practice professionals for more than two decades, we have learned a few key facts:

- No matter what firm the work with – or for – at their core, the men and women who operate at professional level are ultimately self-employed, in that their careers are their number-one clients. This is also true, even for those who are members of large Medical Practice groups. Regardless of the name on the door, ultimately, their success – if any – rests with their own efforts.

- Successful professionals are constantly looking for new prospects, and constantly working to convert those prospects into new patients. They know that to sit still is to lose ground to those with a bit more energy and drive – they live by Abraham Lincoln's famous observation:

  > *"Things may come to those who wait …*
  > *but only the things left by those who hustle …"*

- With the exception of telephones replacing telegraphs, and email replacing surface mail, nothing has really changed in the way professionals have sought new patients since the first stock exchange was set up when, on May 17, 1792, twenty-four brokers met under a buttonwood tree in lower Manhattan to create what became the New York Stock Exchange. Regardless of the nature of the profession, personal and professional reputation is at the heart of their success.

- Successful professionals also know there's got to be a better way – they are constantly looking for a new approach to finding prospects, then converting them into patients.

Which brings us to the point.

If you're a private-practice professional, and if you're reading this book, you know the value of hustling for prospects and patients – you know that if you don't do it or see that it gets done, nobody's going to do it for you. You also know that your professional reputation – and often your personal reputation – are your most valuable assets.

If you're known and trusted, half the job's done – but if you're relatively unknown, mere hustling may not be enough. To bridge that gap, you know how to network and you know how to man the phones, but you also know that networking and cold calling are inherently, inefficiently retail – an approach that is as time-consuming and costly as it is ultimately, reliably effective.

As skilled as you are with traditional business-building networking approaches, you want something more efficient, more cost-effective and – over time – even more reliable than that reliably old-fashioned approach to sales.

Traditionally, that old-fashioned approach has meant burning a lot of shoe leather, and burning up a lot of phone lines, attending community events and other civic club meetings, buying a lot of meals and playing a lot of golf – all hoping to network yourself into yet another client, a referral arrangement or a business deal.

If you know how to make this time-honored networking drill work, this does remain an effective way of attracting prospects (as noted earlier in the book), but it is hardly efficient or cost-effective. Besides, it's what everybody does – and when you're doing what everybody does, it's hard to stand apart as someone special.

Internet Marketing, Blogs, and Social Networking – The New Technology Alternative

Thanks to the Internet – including websites and blogs and Social Media networking sites such as Facebook and LinkedIn, YouTube and Twitter – it is now possible to set yourself apart from the herd, and to do so without leaving your office. Social Media make possible a relatively new kind of networking – one called Social Networking. If you do it right, social networking sets you apart as Subject Matter Expert – someone who others turn to for answers – or even a "Thought Leader," someone people turn to for leadership.

By providing content and communications, you can become someone who, in a relatively narrow area of expertise, is seen by others as being a step ahead of the pack, someone worth listening to.

A Subject Matter Expert. A Thought Leader.

Before delving into the details of Internet Marketing, first, here's a brief introduction to the five secrets of Internet Marketing success that – when applied properly, create certain success:

Content: Create and present new and readily-accessible free information, "content," that is different enough to be engaging. This sets you apart. However, make sure that your content is frequently refreshed – you need to create enough ongoing and useful content to be sure that the people who ought to be interested in what you have to say keep coming back for more.

Conversation: Unlike a speech you gave at a community event – or even a book you wrote as an acknowledged expert – Blogging and Social Networking is not all about a top-down preaching effort. Rather, when done right, Blogging and Social Networking are more akin to a virtual peer-to-peer dialog ... on steroids. To succeed, you need to not just create and present content – you must monitor this for responses from others, then answer those responses you generate. In time, you'll find yourself at the center of a conversation.

Visualize it – it should look like the expanding rings you create when you chuck a rock into a still pond – and these echoes, as they expand, bring you to the attention of people who may have missed your initial content.

Consistency: To be successful in Blogging and Social Networking, you need to make a commitment to post both regularly and frequently. Occasional posts issued at odd intervals are insufficient for the creation of "followers" (see below) – and those followers are essential.

Each tool (see below for details) needs its own frequency. Though more often is better, major White Paper can be issued just six times per year and still be effective; however, blogs should be issued once a week and Tweets and Facebook should be published two to three times per week.

Set a pace that is both comfortable and sustainable – if you find that even this is a challenge, look for a "ghost-writer" who can help you sustain the consistent frequency – as well as the quality – needed to grab and hold that Subject Matter Expert or Thought Leader position.

Followers: These are people who, having become interested in your content contributions, will formally identify themselves as friends (Facebook), followers (Twitter, LinkedIn) or subscribers (YouTube). Followers will become part of your virtual, online network – your personal Social Network – if you offer both useful content and vibrant two-way conversation.

These followers – at least those who are the right people (i.e., potential prospects or referral sources) – will become engaged with you, even if only in their own minds, and they will then network out to their own friends and followers and spread the word ... the word about you – Subject Matter Expert or Thought Leader – and your useful, fresh and original content.

Transformation: This is the inevitable process inherent in effective Social Networking – the process of turning followers and friends into prospects, lead-sources or patients. To be ultimately effective in Social Networking (Facebook, Twitter, LinkedIn, Google Plus, Pinterest) - unless this is just an ego trip (which it often is, but not for people who become financially successful because of their online efforts) – you've got to monetize your followers, based on the content and the conversation, in a way that makes the creation of free content worth it. If you're an investment agent, broker or advisor, this ultimately means new patients.

When you've embraced *these five secrets of Blogging and Social Networking success*, you will have created for yourself a persona as a Subject Matter Expert or even a Thought Leader. You will have transformed yourself, in your online persona – in your own special area of expertise – into someone who people looking for answers will turn to for advice, insight and business support.

That's the initial, primary goal of your Blogging and Social Networking efforts. Once you're seen as a Subject Matter Expert or Thought Leader, a content expert, a "guru," you should have no trouble turning followers into prospects, and prospects into patients.

Keep this in mind – nobody will become a follower unless they have a personal interest in your area of specialization. Some followers will be colleagues, for sure, but most will be potential patients who are looking for reliable answers to very specific questions.

If you answer those questions, you'll earn their trust. They will then turn – as prospects always do – to someone they trust to provide the services they're looking for.

Getting Practical
Tools for Transformation

To become a Thought Leader, even before you start producing the content that will lead people to find you, you'll need to create several essential Blogging and Social Networking **infrastructure tools**. These include:

- A **website** – pick a URL that reflects yourself, your business and your proposed Thought Leadership position (such as www.c-level-exec-pro.com or www.professional-practice-expert.com), then create the site in your persona as Thought Leader, then populate it with initial copy reflecting this expertise. See below for an outline of such a website.

- An **email address**, linked to the URL, so you can communicate in the persona to be created by the website.

- A **blog-site** on Blogger or WordPress – each has benefits and shortcomings – however, Blogger (www.blogger.com) is both easier to use and linked to Google (the parent company) ensuring that it will be easily "searched."

- A **Facebook BUSINESS account** (which is different from the personal account). When you create the Business Account, make sure that your personal account – assuming you have one – isn't sharply at odds with the business one. Too many people sabotage their business image by portraying a playboy image on their Facebook personal account. Remember, if you put it online, they will find it.

  In addition, you can use Facebook to create competitions that bring interested parties to your site, and ultimately to your practice. As the saying goes, "don't try this at home." Engage an expert in this field, which changes at the speed of light, to ensure your best chance for success.

- A **Twitter** account, linked to the Facebook BUSINESS account. Using a Facebook app, you can link the two accounts together, so Tweets to your Twitter Followers will also reach your Facebook friends. As noted above, the "conversation" is critical to Social Networking success, and both Twitter and Facebook are ideal forums for engaging in the "conversation."

- A **LinkedIn** account – LinkedIn is more business-oriented than is Facebook – though not as popular or widely used. It is an excellent place to network, and it is ideal as a means of establishing your Thought Leadership position.

- **Google +, Pinterest and Instagram** – are a growing social networks that we are finding useful.

- **Apps:** An increasing number of retail businesses – including physician Medical Practices and med-spas, are creating Apps that link consumers to themselves via the consumers' own smart phones. There are an abundance of qualified App developers in the US and especially in India, and the costs for development are no longer out of line with their potential for positive marketing impact.

- **Google searches** related to our parallel topics to keep posted on breaking news, blog posts, etc. You will want to seek out others who blog on your subjects – then periodically add thoughtful and respectful comments (respectful especially if you disagree) to their own blogs. This is part of the "conversation" noted above.

- A **YouTube** network set up to host videos, should you choose to venture into the realm of video blogs (highly recommended IF you can present yourself well on camera). If you have stage fright, or are uncomfortable reading your blog on camera, don't go the YouTube route – but if you're comfortable in front of others – perhaps as a platform speaker – then YouTube is a "must."

There may be other infrastructure tools you'll need later on, but to begin the process, this should be sufficient.

For instance, once you've created a strong pool of committed followers, you may want to look at installing a "Buddy Press" captive social network within the website.

Buddy Press is a useful free tool created by the WordPress folks that allows you to create a virtual affinity group (i.e., a business "fan club") on your website – but that is definitely a "down the road" addition useful only to those who are truly committed to an aggressive implementation of Social Media methods and tactics.

Implementing and Improving
Your Social Networking Tools

Blogging and Social Networking are essential, but it's time-consuming. With the Internet replacing the Yellow Pages, you've got to be there, and prominently, if you want to succeed. With such a priority, and with so much time involved, it is often better to turn your blogging and social networking over to an expert than to try to do it, half-heartedly, in your meager spare time, on your own.

To put these foundational tools into place, here are the steps you'll need to follow:

Create a plan of action – including the topics you'll cover, the frequency of your various posts, the signposts you'll look for on the road to success, etc. This does not need to be detailed, but it will prove useful in keeping you focused.

Create the foundational tools noted above, then begin creating basic content for the sites as needed.

White Papers and Case Studies (and video versions):

- On a schedule identified in the Plan, write periodic White Papers or Case Study of from five to twenty-five pages, each focused on a specific portion of the expertise that will, collectively, elevate you into thought leadership. If you're not entirely clear on what, exactly, constitutes a Case Study or a White Paper, consider that what you're reading right now was originally published as a White Paper.

  Note the style, the outline (major sections, sub-sections), and the pacing. Note how this takes you from broad concept to specific details – then adapt the outline and approach to your own subject matter.

- Use graphic layout and letterhead to give some formality to the White Paper or Case Study. Don't be shy about including graphics if these are appropriate. Include your contact information and hot-link URLs to your website and blog site (see below).

- Produce the White Papers and Case Studies as PDF documents (to make them less likely to be modified and "borrowed" without permission) and note on them that they can be reprinted or used (without change) with permission, to encourage others to share them widely.

- Offer them as free downloads from your website – and include a link to them in your blogs, especially blogs based on the White Papers and Case Studies.

eBooks: Publishing and distributing eBooks will position you as an "author" in a way that blogs and White Papers can never do. Both prospects/patients and even the news media will see you as inherently more credible for having published books.

- Pull together a collection of White Papers (minimum 36-50 pages when paginated, with lengths up to 250 pages possible) into a thematic eBook that will then be offered as free downloaded content.

- Lay the text out in book format (pagination, illustrations, cover, etc.) – and don't be shy about using graphs, used-with-permission photos and other illustrations to dress up the eBook.

- Post eBooks for free downloads – these become the ultimate in free content, as well as a great credibility builder

- Down the road, you can pull together a set of from three to five eBooks into the manuscript for a full-length to-be-published printed book. This book would be offered as both a not-free printed and e-book published book. Do this only if you believe that the printed book will either be a useful sales tool or if you honestly believe that the printed book would sell in quantities sufficient to justify the printing costs.

PR and Press Releases

- Create under-400-word press releases to announce your White Papers – this will help attract readers and build your reputation at the same time.

- Set up a free account for BusinessWire, then use this fee-based service for distributing press releases promoting your White Papers – and, down the road, your eBooks. Do not use a "national" distribution – ask them for the most local (and most inexpensive) geographic distribution for your release.

- If you have no experience in placing press releases, ask your BusinessWire account representative to walk you through the process – they are unfailingly helpful and willing to work with you.

- PR – use professional Public Relations techniques to help generate followers and online "buzz" for your thought leadership White Papers, eBooks and Blogs. Here are some PR techniques you can use.

- o   Monitor breaking news in your thought leadership niche-market news space

- o   Write and post short, pithy blogs related to breaking news you find

- o   If you also use video blogs as well as written blogs, create video blogs related to breaking news and post them on YouTube and your website

- o   Seek out others' blogs writing in your thought leadership niche market space (use Google Search to find them) and comment on them as appropriate

Blogs: These blogs will be the core of your ongoing communications with your followers and friends, as well as those who might become followers down the road. While White Papers and eBooks are 'bigger' and 'more impressive,' blogs are your most important thought-leadership communications tools.

In these, you'll take elements of White Papers, or breaking news, or some "issue" and articulate your views in chunks of 250-to-300 words – short enough to be easily read, yet long enough to make an important point, one worth reading and remembering. Here's how to proceed:

- • Write a set of blogs, based on each Case Study or White Paper, that break it down into bite-sized thought-chunks. Typically, a ten-page White Paper will yield half a dozen useful blogs, each visiting in a more conversational tone one of the important points within the White Paper. Sometimes, a White Paper might yield as many as 25 blogs – but for that, you'll need a longer and more detailed White Paper.

- • When we write blogs for our patients based on White Papers, we typically write all of the appropriate blogs, based on the White Papers, as soon as the White Paper has its final edit, and before we post it. We also generally write the two or three promotional tweets that go with each blog at the time we write these client blogs, then load the Tweets into TweetDeck (see below) to be issued at a later date. While we don't use them, there are tools available for managing and scheduling the posting of blogs, such as Hootsuite, which work a lot like TweetDeck.

- Write blogs based on breaking news and other relevant topics not linked to the White Papers. Because business and the professions are heavily-regulated and intimately linked to national economic recovery initiatives, you might be tempted to write politically-themed blog-posts. Remember, some patients may not share your political beliefs – so venture into this realm cautiously, eyes-open.

- Should you venture into creating political blog-posts, you can create a parallel blog-site at Townhall.com to more effectively reach the political audience likely to be interested in an investment agent, broker or advisor's views of the implications of state and federal regulation of investment products and services.

- Seek out investment-related blog-sites and either create a parallel blog-site within that domain or offer "guest blog" posts to the blog-sites. This is an excellent way of spreading the word – and you can often just re-publish previously-created blogs – and attracting new followers.

Video Blogs: As noted above, you should not venture into video blogs unless you're comfortable in front of a camera. In video blogs, white board presentation or other video, style is as important as substance (something you won't face in printed blogs), so only use this if you can create a good, straightforward and technically-competent video, and only if you're comfortable and effective on camera. No video blog is infinitely preferable to no video blog at all.

- If you go the video route, in addition to posting them on your website, create a YouTube network to house your growing collection of videos

- Create video blogs based on written blogs – including both White Paper-linked blogs and breaking-news blogs

- Invite satisfied patients to create testimonial blogs – these are far more powerful than printed testimonials, and far more believable as well. Post them on YouTube and on your website

- A new online video technology, Google Hangouts – initially appearing to be a "Super Skype" with connections for up to ten individuals –

seems to offer potential for video consults and small-group presentations. It's still new, and experts are still trying to figure out how to turn it into a social networking and marketing tool, but it's one to keep your eye on.

Blog Comments: Commenting on others' social media posts is an important and effective way of attracting new friends-and-followers online, by showcasing your insights in front of audiences others have already created for their social media posts and/or linked blogs. Only comment on social media posts that are in the same basic market niche you're embracing as a fledgling thought leader – don't shotgun this approach.

- First, use Google Search and Twitter to find others who are blogging on your niche-market topic area.

- Monitor those social media posts – looking for opportunities to offer intelligent comments.

- Whenever appropriate, comment on the social media posts – see below for how to comment.

- Monitor these social media posts and your comments for further comments, and remain engaged – if someone answers you, engage that comment with one of your own.

- Remain professional in all comments – don't be drawn into an emotional debate.

- In every comment, you want to advance the discussion. Either agree with the host social media post, then add a useful additional point or two – or, respectfully disagree and make from one to three brief points. Don't ramble, don't filibuster, and don't pontificate. Show respect, show insights, back up your statements and remain conversational.

Ongoing Twitter Activity: As noted above, post Tweets, as well as comments on Facebook and LinkedIn. This should be a daily – ideally a several-times-daily – process for Twitter, at least three times a week for Facebook and three times a week for LinkedIn. These should cover the following – remember, you're part of a conversation:

- From one to three (per day) Tweets and posts offering brief insights into your primary topic, based on your professionalism

- At least once a day, create one Tweet and other posts with a link to a third-party source offering information you'd like to share

- Retweet at least one useful post a day – five would be better, as it keeps you engaged, but once per day is the minimum.

- Post at least one "personal" (i.e., not professional) account per day. This doesn't have to be "intimately personal" – in fact, it shouldn't be. However, the point is to show your humanity. Some recent effective personal Tweets I've posted include the note that Reno had freezing rain and snow-covered mountains in all directions, and another was a link to a particularly funny cartoon. Your goal here is to humanize yourself to your friends and followers.

- At least once a day – and as often as you can justify it – tweet a respond-all comment to one of the people you follow. This really helps advance the idea that Social Networking is all about the conversation.

- Always reply to everyone who replies to you. This is common courtesy, as well as the best possible way of keeping the conversation moving forward.

More on Twitter: There are tools available – some free, such as TweetDeck, and some with nominal fees, such as HootSuite – which allow you to manage your tweeting to control the time it takes. Here are a few hints:

- Using TweetDeck to post ongoing professional-tips tweets (we post three-per-day during weekdays and once mid-day Saturdays), and load them in a month in advance, freeing our staff up to concentrate on the more timely tweets and reducing my overall time.

- We have client Twitter accounts linked to our smart phones, allowing us to monitor, post and reply to Tweets even when we're away from our office and computer.

- We have our client Twitter account linked to their Facebook accounts, so all of their Tweets populate their Facebook accounts as well. Of course, we post other items on their Facebook pages which aren't Tweeted, but in this way we generate more content on Facebook (which reaches a different audience) without additional effort.

Work LinkedIn forums/discussions related to your primary Thought Leader market-niche topic focus, adding comments, starting threads and engaging in the conversation there.

Create an email database of followers who opt-in for emails by contacting you on your website (as well as those who give you business cards at real-world networking events).

- Send them links to White Papers, blogs and other content products (including video blogs).

- Periodically encourage them to follow you on various social media.

- Issue special breaking-news alerts (keep your followers apprised via email as well as social media of what's happening in your market-niche Thought Leader space).

Website: Though it's listed last – because it's not a new "Social Networking" concept – your website must be at the heart of your online (and off-line) marketing and promotional efforts. If you don't already have a website, in the beginning keep it simple and to the point.

If you already have a website, and you should, take a moment to review the content recommended below, then ensure that your existing website includes this material. If you don't have a website, use this as a conceptual template for creating one at FatCow or GoDaddy or one of the other improbably-named hosting sites that provides easy-to-use, plug-and-play website templates.

- **Home Page** – here you present basic information about you and your services, along with links to the major sub-pages (which tie into your Social Networking efforts).

    o Who you are

- What you do

- Who you serve

- What you offer

A Page Link Menu (on your home page) will link visitors to all of the other pages noted below

- About you and your vision (your position) – this defines who you are as a business person – it is the essence of who you are in the eyes of your patients and prospects.

- Product Page – Samples of What You Provide (links or downloadable as PDFs) of the services you offer as an Investment professional

- Photo gallery pages with each photo carefully labeled

- Social Networking Communications Tools: Here you link to or provide downloads for your Social Networking tools:

  - White Papers (pdf downloads) and eBooks (when available)

  - Case Studies

  - Blogs

  - Video blogs

  - Blog Comments

  - Twitter and Facebook and LinkedIn (encourage visitors to follow you on these various sites)

- Testimonial Page – Kudos and endorsements

- E-Commerce Page – buy now! – this would apply if you have something to sell online for example your own product line or gift cards

- Contact – how to get hold of you

Conclusion – Getting It Right

Internet Marketing is not hard if you're used to writing, networking and selling yourself – and also educating the lay public on your areas of specialization. Social Networking is all about content and communications. If you want to become a Subject Matter Expert or Thought Leader, you already have the intellectual tools to do it. What you need now is the commitment to carry forward – which means regular communications.

Unless you hand off the actual creation of the content and the placement of the blogs and posts to a "virtual ghost-writer" – someone in your employ or an outside consultant – you have to commit to creating content on the schedule noted above. You also have to commit to spending time each day on Twitter, Facebook and LinkedIn. Rather than this being a chore, you may soon find that it's a pleasure – potentially even an addictive pleasure (and at that point, the challenge will be to control and limit your time online, rather than finding time to post and monitor your posts).

However, the payoff is remarkable. You can be seen as a Thought Leader within a matter of weeks or months (depending on how regular and frequent you make your posts), and from there, it is a short step to creating fans, advocates, referral sources, prospects and patients – and more business. Remember, this is a business venture, rather than a game or a play-time. It is far less costly than traditional advertising – or even public relations – and the results can be all out of proportion with your cost investment, or even your time investment.

But it's up to you – more than any other kind of marketing except for face-to-face networking – success in Social Networking depends on your interest and your commitment.

OK, So You Received a Rotten Review

Now, What Do You Do?

"Dr. Smith was arrogant, insensitive, and ran late. The diagnosis he gave me was wrong. And for that, I had to dish out $50 co-pay. Stay away."

Most doctors go into medicine to help patients. Some doctors do provide better care than others. But, most are conscientious and wake up every day intending to do the best possible job for their patients.

The average doctor sees between 1,000 and 3,000 patients each year. Despite their best efforts, it is impossible to make 100% of your patients happy. Because of the prevalence of the Internet, that makes it inevitable you will, at some point, receive a bad online review.

It could be for any number of reasons, or for no reason at all. Still, it's there. Google will find it. Patients will find it. Prospective patients will find it.

What to do? Here we offer you five "take home points" that, if followed, will help reduce negative reviews and put the ones that remain in context.

First, take a deep breath. If it's an isolated rotten review, amidst a sea of positive reviews, that is a very different situation than having scores of rotten reviews. With a few exceptions, the public generally understands you cannot make everyone happy.

But, the public also expects you will make most patients happy, and everybody holds doctors to a higher standard – after all, you hold their health and even their lives in your hands.

So, **take-home point #1:** Do not sweat an isolated negative review.

Next, do you know who the patient is and can you fix the problem?

Most reviews are anonymous – especially the negative reviews – and based on the nature of the site and the review, you may not have specific information to allow you to determine who wrote it.

However, if you can decipher the review and identify the author, consider reaching out to that patient. If you can possibly fix the patient's problem, do so.

Sometimes, a negative review can be triggered by something as simple as an escalating misunderstanding over a $20 bill. Other times, it's the perception that you were rude or did not listen. These are solvable issues.

In many instances, merely calling the patient and apologizing for a misunderstanding may be enough. Since most doctors do not call their patients about such matters – when YOU do so, it sets you apart from others.

This is what top performers in every other industry do. Healthcare should not be an exception.

Take-home point #2: If can identify the patient, communicate with that person and do your best to solve the problem.

Sometimes, however, you are not sure who the patient is. The complaint is general. If it's a systemic complaint about your office, and you can fix it – do so. Then, tell the world you heard the message and took action.

If it's an isolated complaint, consider responding online. However, you will need to pay attention to HIPAA. Even though the patient may not have posted a name, the post may contain enough details in the post to identify the patient.

Be careful.

Take-home point #3: Consider responding online to the post if you can do so in a HIPAA compliant form.

Every review site is its own "ecosystem." They have their own guiding philosophies and rules. Most have *Terms of Use*. If you believe the review was unfair, that it violated the terms of use, diplomatically write the site and ask if it will take a look at the post in the context of its own rules.

They may agree with you and remove the post.

Remember, each site is run by people, just like you. They are more likely to respond to "please" and "thank you" than threats. Couch your note as a request and not a demand.

Take-home point #4: Review sites may remove an unfair post if it violates its Terms of Use.

Finally, a high-performing practice can be distinguished online by proactively asking your patients for feedback. If you have a great patient safety record, positive clinical outcomes, and great "customer service", your online reputation should mirror your actual reputation.

However, to be successful here, you have to be diligent in asking your patients for online feedback. When the inevitable negative review does surface, it will be placed in context of the multitude of positives.

Take-home point #5: Asking your patients proactively for online feedback – this allows high-performing practices to be fairly represented online.   This also drives new patient volume and new patient revenue.

If you practice medicine, you will occasionally receive a bad – indeed even a rotten – review. The best way to prepare for that day is to actively ask your patients for online feedback each and every day.

That way you will defined by hundreds of your satisfied patients instead of two noisy patients with megaphones – and the public will have a representative picture of your practice.

Section Four – Ghost Writing

Ghost Writing and Social Networking

One of the most immediate and effective ways of turning a physician into a "Subject Matter Expert" or "Thought Leader" within their areas of professional expertise is to create and publish a book or eBook. For a variety of reasons, both members of the news media and members of the public at large are eager to grant enhanced credibility to the authors of non-fiction books or eBooks.

Hiring a ghost writer will use the written word to position you as an online guru. You'll be seen as a "subject matter expert," someone who others will turn to, when considering aesthetic medical or spa services.

Among both patients and the news media, there are few people who are more credible than published authors. Ghost writer's help patients not only become published book authors, but they also develop those books in a way that attracts patients and generates online buzz long before the books are published.

We recommend the exclusive "Pyramid Approach" to writing published books and eBooks – and in fact, we followed a modified version of that process in creating this book you're now reading:

- First, you need to work with a writer to create a book concept and title that will attract patients or patients, and then break this concept down into a detailed chapter outline. Before you start writing, you know exactly what will be in your book.

- Next, the writer will conduct a series of interviews to identify your perspective on each section and chapter of the book. While the writer will write your book, it will be based on your ideas, insights and expertise.

- Next, the writer will begin writing, publishing and promoting a series of blogs, based on those interviews. These blogs will begin to position you as an expert, as well as the author of your forthcoming book. By publishing and promoting these blogs, you will attract a following and start to generate leads, referrals and new business.

- Then, using the material from several blogs, the writer will write, publish and promote a series of white papers and case studies. They will present the same information, but in a different format, one that appeals to a different audience. These will also position you as both an expert and as the author of your forthcoming book. This will also extend your following and increase your leads, referrals and new business.

- Next, the writer will take the material they've previously written in your blogs, white papers and case studies and repurpose that material, turning it into chapters for your soon-to-be-published book or eBook.

- Finally, they will effectively promote your new book – and, in the process, solidify your position as a subject matter expert and online guru. You will use both social networking and public relations tools to make sure your book or eBook reaches the proper audiences.

This process will also position you as an expert with the news media, helping to generate even more coverage and more target-audience awareness, all leading to leads, referrals and new business.

This book will be yours, representing your expertise, your personality and your goals for your Medical Practice or business. However, instead of having to write your book yourself, the ghost writer will take that burden off of you. You'll receive all the benefits, but without all the work.

Ghost Writing Solutions for eBooks, White Papers and Research Studies

Using Professional Writers to Grow Your Aesthetic Medical Practice ...

Introduction – the New Yellow Pages

Google searches have replaced the Yellow Pages as the primary way in which consumers find the goods and services they need. This fact-of-life now includes cosmetic surgery, aesthetics-oriented med-spas, cosmetic dermatology, anti-aging services, wellness programs and other professionals who provide appearance-enhancing services to consumers.

Websites remain critical for business development, but they are no longer enough. To go along with websites, successful practitioners must provide "content" – white papers, research studies and even ebooks – as potential patients delve into the realm of online communications.

Online marketing communications sites form the channel between a business or professional practice and a potential patient or client. However, this is not about tweets or Facebook posts. It's about serious, informative content – eBooks, white papers, research study write-ups, blogs and video blogs, and other in-depth consumer-oriented information – which gives the potential client or patient confidence.

Along with blogs and video blogs, white papers, case studies – and yes, even eBooks – are the route-markers on your road-map to aesthetic business success in the digital age.

Specifically, to succeed here, you must create sufficient well-written content to not only attract attention one time, but to motivate people to keep coming back to your content sites for new insights into topics that interest your prospective new patients. However, even for the more gifted writers among aesthetic medical practitioners and med-spa managers, creating this kind of regular and frequent – and high-quality – content is a time-consuming challenge.

Such content is necessary, but creating that content may also take more time than can be spared from running the Medical Practice or business and treating patients.

Fortunately, as we have discovered at **beautiful forever** on behalf of our busy professional patients, there is a useful and effective alternative to writing this material – and that alternative is the professional content-development ghost writer. An effective ghost writer can produce white papers, research study findings, case studies, testimonials and even eBooks, freeing business owners and medical professionals to do what they do best, while still creating the content they need to attract new business clients and patients.

Online "Positioning"

One of the most immediate and effective ways of becoming a "Subject Matter Expert" or "Thought Leader" within a given areas of professional expertise involves creating valuable, consumer-or patient-oriented content.

This is built around creating and publishing insightful in-depth white papers and case studies, and research findings. Taken to its logical conclusion, this content development often includes writing and publishing books or eBooks. All of this should be written to reach consumers and potential patients, rather than professional colleagues, and that can become a challenge for individuals used to writing only for their peers.

While medical aesthetic consumers are increasingly fascinated by and attracted to content, which includes – but goes far beyond – well-written blogs and well-presented video blogs. For a variety of reasons, both members of the news media and members of the public at large are eager to grant enhanced credibility to the authors of books or eBooks.

Despite the potential intimidation factor of putting words on a page, these online content tools are not hard to create. Any aesthetic physician or medical spa manager knows enough more about the subject than even the most knowledgeable reporters, editors or consumers. If aesthetics professionals don't have time to write – or sufficient interest in the process of writing lucidly for target market consumers – they still know enough more than their potential readers to be able to work with a professional ghost writer to create what is needed.

Such content is necessary, but creating that content may also take more time than can be spared from running the Medical Practice or business and treating patients.

Fortunately, as we have discovered at *beautiful forever* on behalf of our busy professional clients, there is a useful and effective alternative to writing this material – and that alternative is the professional content-development ghost writer. An effective ghost writer can produce white papers, research study findings, case studies, testimonials and even eBooks, freeing business owners and medical professionals to do what they do best, while still creating the content they need to attract new business clients and patients.

In marketing-oriented content production, it is possible to use the same basic material in several platforms. Each eBook, white paper or research study, for instance, should lead to the creation of a series of blogs. Each blog should also become the basis for one or more video blogs, allowing the same information to reach multiple targets. Some people prefer to read, while others prefer the video approach – by blending the two, you get the best of both worlds.

In addition, each white paper or case study can become "fodder" for a series of shorter and more informal (in style) blogs and video blogs. Finally, the material developed in blogs, white papers, case studies and other online content can be repackaged and enhanced, then used as the basis for books or eBooks.

In this way, your blogs and other content are providing a trial run for key concepts, before they become the basis of a book. In addition, you'll get feedback and input that will strengthen the final product. Finally, by building one on the other, you cut down on research efforts, while still getting maximum utility out of the material you create.

Each of these content items – blog, video blog, white paper, case study, eBook – should also be promoted to the world via both media relations/press releases and via Medical Practice or business marketing posts on well-traveled online sites and information platforms. In this way, maximum exposure for core concepts is achieved.

This process of content creation and promotion will also position the named author with the news media, helping to generate even more coverage and more target-audience awareness, all leading to leads, referrals and new business.

The key to that success, unless you have the time and inclination to be your own writer, is to secure the services of your very own Boswell, someone who will put your thoughts and insights into writing, in ways that can and will enhance your global effort toward marketing, promotion and Medical Practice/business building.
If you'd like more information on ghost writing or how marketing-and business development-oriented content can build your business or Medical Practice, my staff and I would be glad to help.

The Mechanics of Ghost Writing

Before you start looking for a ghost writer, you need to determine if you need a ghost writer – and if so, why. This will help in the selection process. There are two basic reasons for using a ghost writer:

1. You don't feel confident in your own writing ability – your specialty is cosmetic surgery, not word-smithing.

2. You don't have the time to write – there are only 24 hours in a day, and between Medical Practice demands, family and a social life, you don't have time to write what needs to be written.

Once you've determined that you need a ghost writer, decide exactly what that ghost writer is supposed to do for you. A professional ghost is your stand-in, they are writing your thoughts, in your voice, and in your name. This is different from a public relations or advertising copywriter. Ghost writing is personal.

Tasks for which you need a ghost writer include blogs, books, bylined magazine articles and speeches. The key is that the words and ideas are yours, and the pro-ghost is merely putting them into written words for you.

Once you've decided that you need a ghost writer – and know what that ghost is going to write for you – it's time to find the best writer for you. The key here is a personal one – the writer is going to be your voice to the world – he or she needs to be able to write in your voice, to be able to capture your ideas and put them into words that sound like you.

It helps if the writer has done this before, and can show you samples of blogs, or a chapter from a book, or a speech that was written for someone like you.

Reviewing these clips will help you see that the writer has been able to capture your voice and ideas, and put them into words.

Now it gets personal. It's time to find out if you can work with this person – and that's all about chemistry, not about technical ability. Ask the writer how he goes about capturing his client's voice, and spirit, and ideas. Get them to demonstrate, in a brief interview of you, how they work in the interview process.

You might even ask the writer to craft a single sample blog – 250 to 750 words – on a topic, to demonstrate his ability to capture your thoughts and your voice.

But remember, this person is a professional, just like you – and that means that if you ask for a demonstration that goes beyond showing past clip-samples, he should be compensated for that personalized sample of his interview-to-writing process. This sample is obviously more important if you're looking at a long-term project, such as a book.

If you just need a single blog, the sample will be the work product, and should be paid for.

Finally, if you're ready to work together, comes the big question – what is it going to cost? There is no one-size-fits-all pricing for professional ghost writers. Some write by the hour, and have an hourly rate card based on the amount of work you'll be asking for.

Some writers do this to incentivize patients to keep their edits concise and to the point, to keep the process efficient.

Others work by the project, and they have a rate card based on the nature of the project.

Charges range from the very low – for amateurs who are doing this on the side – to the high-end for pro-ghosts who've done this a lot and know what they're doing. In many cases, price-shopping is counterproductive – low rates buy you inexperienced writers, some still using "training wheels" – while high rates may buy you a level of professionalism that exceeds your needs.

The writer who ghost-wrote Lee Iacocca's best-selling book is exceedingly good, but exceedingly expensive – you can probably make do with a professional who has experience, but not that much experience. On the other side of the coin, you've got the stay-at-home-mom who always wanted to write, but who's never done this before.

She may be a diamond in the rough, but do you want to be the one who teaches her the ropes.

It is likely best to find someone who has ghost written for doctors and healthcare professionals – preferably in the aesthetics field. Some PR and ad copywriters can do ghost work, but many cannot – so seek out someone who's done this before, and who understands how to make it happen. This person will have a work schedule planned out – they will know what your time commitment will be, whether he's writing a series of short blogs, or an entire book.

Bottom line – if you want a ghost writer, you want someone who's been there and done that – a professional. You'll want someone skilled in writing in your voice, and in capturing your ideas and putting them into words. You'll want someone you're comfortable working with, and someone who respects the restrictions on your time, and who can work within those restrictions.

Section Five: Books and eBooks

The following is an adaptation of an eBook we developed on how to write books and eBooks – it is presented here for the first time in published form.

Creating Published Books and eBooks to Cost-Effectively Promote Your Medical Practice

Introduction

Over the past decade, effective Social Networking – making professional use of Social Media, from Facebook and Twitter to YouTube, LinkedIn and Pinterest – has emerged as both one of the lowest cost and most effective ways of marketing a professional aesthetics Medical Practice, spa or other related business.

The keys to this success focus around positioning the leading practice professional as an internet guru, a recognized "Subject Matter Expert" or even a "Thought Leader" within the Social Networking realm. Then – once that positioning has been accomplished – using Social Networking techniques to translate that positioning and recognition into marketing goals.

These include goals such as attracting new clients, or increasing the use of the practice's products and services among existing patients.

One of the most immediate and effective ways of turning a physician or aesthetician into a "Subject Matter Expert" or "Thought Leader" within their areas of professional expertise is to create and publish a book or eBook.

For a variety of reasons, both members of the news media and members of the public at large are eager to grant enhanced credibility to the authors of non-fiction books or eBooks.

However, the idea of writing a book – or even a published book or eBook – seems daunting to many otherwise competent professionals.

Unlike the thought of writing a blog, a guest editorial – or even a white paper or case study – the sheer challenge of writing an entire book often seems intimidating. However, it does not need to be.

The following step-by-step guide illustrates a simple, yet comprehensive process that we have created, one that will help them become both published book authors and highly-regarded Social Media subject-matter experts.

We refer to this as our exclusive "Social Networking Foundation Approach" to creating published books or eBooks. This is because of the way we guide you to build the chapters of your book out of a carefully-planned series of blogs, white papers and case studies.

Using our "Social Networking Foundation Approach," you'll be presenting different audiences the same basic information, but in different formats that meet different audiences' information needs.

There are a remarkable number of benefits to our "Social Networking Foundation Approach," which we will also present in this guide.

However, this is not a quick-and-dirty "Cliff's Notes" overview of our customized process.

Instead, you will find that we have created for you an in-depth description of a foolproof approach for significantly growing your professional practice or aesthetics business.

In developing this approach, we have written more than a dozen published books on healthcare and aesthetics marketing, public relations, advertising and promotion – including the book you're reading now – as well as ghost written books for clients, many of them physicians or surgeons. We have given dozens of webinars and state-of-the-art presentations at professional society meetings.

And, most important, we have successfully marketed and promoted literally scores of aesthetics Medical Practices, products and product lines, spas and other related aesthetics businesses, and we've been doing so for nearly three decades.

All of that successful experience has been distilled into this practical, in-depth guide.

Once you've read and digested this step-by-step guide, you will have at your fingertips everything that you need to know in order to create Social Networking success on your own.

In the following pages, we will first lay out the basics of Social Networking – then we will guide you on a logical and easy-to-implement process that will transform you into a Subject Matter Expert and Thought Leader, one who will attract both new patients and repeat business, and one who will earn referrals from clients, patients and business associates.

About Social Networking: Social Networking communications are comprised of two elements: "**content**" and "**conversation**."

"**Content**" – including White Papers, Case Studies, Blogs, Video Blogs, Blog Comments, Webinars and other forms of information – is what brings readers (or viewers) to your Social Media pages. More important, if the content adds real value to members of your audience, it brings them back.

"**Conversation**" – including Tweets, Facebook and LinkedIn posts and other forms of conversation – is what humanizes Social Networking. More important, if conversation posts are effective, they turn your readers or viewers into followers and fans.

The effective combination of "Content" and "Conversation" is what turns a Social Networker into a "Subject Matter Expert" or "Thought Leader," someone who is cited, referred to, respected and called on for information and insight.

While "conversation" is what humanizes your presence in the world of Social Media, what you produce as content is the basis of your Social Networking success.

To gather followers, before you can dazzle them with your "conversation," you must first have something worth saying – content. Further, to impress potential followers with your content, you must also come up with effective ways of communicating what you have to say.

Content Platforms: Blogs and video blogs, white papers and case studies – even webinars and YouTube videos – all have the potential to succeed as means of presenting content. This is because the huge number of people who use the Internet as their primary source of information are not, in fact, a group.

Rather, they are individuals, people who have very personal preferences for how they receive "content" – as well as their very different preferences for receiving different kinds of content.

For instance, many tens of millions of Americans prefer to read a brief and relatively casual blog, while hundreds of thousands of others actually prefer the more in-depth (and occasionally more scholarly-seeming) approach that typifies white papers.

Still hundreds of thousands of other content readers would rather receive the facts-and-figures – as well as the stated or implied testimonials – that can be found in case studies.

However, a completely different group, made up of tens of millions of social networkers, prefer to obtain their information in a more audio-visual format.

For instance, they prefer watching video blogs to reading printed blogs. In addition, they prefer more in-depth YouTube videos to published white papers, and choose webinars over case studies. This helps to explain why, after Google, the most widely-used search engine is YouTube.

Integrating Content Presentation: The truly successful content communicator makes use of more than one format. Successful bloggers should, for instance, also create parallel video blogs. These should be short on slick and expensive "production values" but long on content.

Though it may seem counter-intuitive, video blogs which feature too "professional" an appearance actually reduces their effectiveness.

These YouTube video blogs, white board videos and webinars also serve a "conversational" function by highlighting the presenters' personalities.

The most successful social networkers will make use of both printed and video content formats, the better to reach the broadest possible audience. By offering choices, you are allowing your audiences to choose for themselves the format which they prefer.

This multi-format approach to content presentation is also inherent in this "Social Networking Foundation Approach" to successful, Medical Practice-building social networking.

Properly done, this approach can also lead to the successful creation of the ultimate and most credible form of "content" – a published book or eBook.

The very thought of creating published books or eBooks has often proved daunting to otherwise successful content creators, in part because the very idea of writing an effective and coherent book-length document seems intimidating. This is especially true for those content creators who are accustomed to writing and presenting complete and cogent thoughts in 750-word (or less) blogs.

However, as the author of more than a dozen published books – and as the ghost-writer of at least that many other books – several years ago, we began to explore ways that bloggers could turn their brief and insightful content into viable and effective published books or eBooks.

Using this Social Networking Foundation Approach, a content creator can easily and painlessly write the blogs, white papers, case studies and other short social networking "content" that will become the basis of a successful published book or eBook – and, as will be shown, this process will also create reader demand for that published book or eBook, even as it's being written in early-draft form.

With this system, by first planning a focused book or eBook – then by creating an outline of that book's eventual chapter-by-chapter (and sub-section by sub-section) content – the actual book content will be created in a series of blogs, white papers, case studies and other, shorter Social Networking documents.

By focusing on individual (and shorter) formats that are already familiar to – and within the comfort zone of – the Social Networker, the stress and anxiety that are often the nemesis of successful first-time book authors becomes irrelevant.

However, this "Social Networking Foundation Approach" goes several steps further.

First, by publishing these carefully planned-out blogs, white papers and case studies in social media's various "content" platforms, the ideas themselves begin to appear online, and – if they're sound and well-written – to develop an online following of readers and fans.

Then, by promoting each of these blogs, case studies and white papers through the social media's "conversation" platforms – including Facebook, LinkedIn, Pinterest and Twitter – awareness of, and later, demand for these online building blocks that will lead to the book or eBook itself will build interest and demand long before the book or eBook itself is completed and published.

Though elements of this approach have been used by others in the past, the careful and planned integration of these various approaches represent something new to the Social Networking world – we're only exaggerating a little when we say that we'd patent this approach if we could …

This innovative and integrated Social Networking Foundation Approach allows content creators to develop, over time, the building blocks of a book. These include a few topical blogs, several focused white papers and a number of on-target case studies. Once these are created, the author – perhaps with our help – strings them together into a book or eBook.

As noted earlier, this distinctive Social Networking Foundation Approach process can, and should, be supported by video blogs, YouTube videos and webinars. These are the audio-visual equivalent of blogs, white papers and case studies, and will further build demand for the book or eBook, long before it's completed and published.

Perhaps most important, this highly-customized Social Networking Foundation Approach has the potential to turn anyone who has specific expertise – as well as the ability to either write effective blogs, or to work with ghost writers or co-writers – into a published book or eBook author. With that book will come all the credibility and respect that being a published author generates.

The Value and Impact of a Published Book or eBook

Whether a published book or eBook has been sold or – as is often the case with eBooks and promotional books – given away, a published book or eBook created using the Social Networking Foundation Approach presented here makes the person who wrote the book or eBook a published author.

For a variety of reasons, both the Social Networking world and the news media respect the named writers of published books. Both groups accord published book authors a level of credibility hard to obtain in other ways.

Even better, as soon as an individual decides to write a published book or eBook, then comes up with at least a provisional title, that person is legitimately "the author of the forthcoming book, *Title*." With that credibility, the writer can begin immediately to experience at least some of the benefits of being a published author.

In addition, each blog, white paper, case study or audio-visual equivalent can legitimately be presented as "based on the forthcoming book, *Title*," giving that shorter-form content added credibility as well. However, the book or eBook can go a lot farther than that in creating both credibility and success.

An excellent example – and one of the role models we used in creating this Social Networking Foundation Approach – is author and PR expert David Meerman Scott. In building his reputation as "the" subject matter expert in the realm of online public relations, Scott first created a free eBook on the emerging subject of "*PR 2.0.*"

In this free-download eBook, Scott presented his new "take" on public relations, an approach that freely and effectively integrates social networking into more traditional public relations. That remarkable and trend-setting eBook was downloaded for free more than 250,000 times, making it something of an eBook sensation.

However, after writing that eBook, Scott expanded and converted the free eBook into a conventionally-published book which, in 2006, became a New York Times business bestseller. Even more remarkable, because of the rapid changes in social networking in the latter half of the last decade, Scott found the need to produce a second and significantly updated second edition – and, remarkably, that second edition also became a New York Times business bestseller.

It's now in its fourth edition, and still selling like the proverbial hotcakes, because it remains the class act in the field (as is Mr. Scott himself).

While Scott has written other marketing and communications books which have also been successful, we believe that it was his 250,000-copy free eBook, followed by his four editions of his New York Times bestseller, which firmly positioned him as a Subject Matter Expert.

He is, arguably, the most recognized Thought Leading innovator in the emerging field which integrates social networking and public relations.

Scott has been able to transform that widespread recognition and respect into a remarkable career as a consultant and worldwide public speaker – as well as a continually successful author and innovator.

David Meerman Scott's example is obviously the "best case scenario," a publishing phenomenon that also became a dynamic career-builder. However, Scott's roadway to success is also, arguably, an effective model for any aspiring book or eBook author.

For instance, in addition to his free-download eBook, *The New Rules of PR – How To Create A Press Release Strategy for Reaching Buyers Directly* – which is still available – he has also converted sections and sub-sections of his books into blogs and other short-form "content."

This abundant online information is easily searchable by topic, and anyone who finds useful information from one of these blogs becomes an instant candidate for purchasing the published version of Scott's *New Rules PR 2.0.* book, along with his other published books.

We have built on the process used by Scott and other online publishing successes to create our Social Networking Foundation Approach. Using this approach – either on your own or with our professional help – you can use your personal and professional knowledge, as well as your writing skill, to become a published book or eBook author.

Even better, you can create your book or eBook quickly and painlessly – and you'll find that the process can be more fun than you'd believe possible.

This Social Networking Foundation Approach will also help you become seen by your followers as guru in your area of professional expertise – a social networking subject-matter expert or thought leader, as well as a published author.

However, don't expect – if you follow this Social Networking Foundation Approach – that you will soon be giving talks all over the world like David Meerman Scott. As we said, that was the ultimate best case scenario. However, whether you write your own book or you work together with co-writers or even ghost-writers, you will quickly become a reputable and well-known – in your field – published author, with all the respect and credibility that status generates.

A Publishing Secret

Most people assume that eBooks are roughly the same length as regularly published books. While this is often the case, a publishing secret is this: published eBooks do not have to be anywhere near as long as a traditionally-published book to be successful.

For instance, David Meerman Scott's seminal and career-building eBook on public relations is just 22 pages long, yet he turned that into a one-man publishing, consulting and public speaking empire.

While there are successful eBooks that run 250 pages – and these are not at all uncommon – there are many successful and well-received business eBooks that run from 25 to 50 pages.

This length is measured in "typeset pages," rather than manuscript pages, but eBooks that run less than 100 manuscript pages are routinely considered "real books" and – if the topic and the writing are on-target – they will be accepted by their readers.

Creating an eBook success isn't dependent on producing Tom Clancy-length books – and that is one of publishing's best-kept secrets. The proper length of an eBook is whatever it takes for you – the author – to make your case on the subject you've selected to address.

The Social Networking Foundation Approach Process

The process itself is simple, and it comes with two variations.

The first – you can do it all yourself. As a physician or aesthetics business owner:

- You already have clear ideas of what you want to say – as well as to whom you want to say it.

- You already know how to organize your thoughts.

- You also have the basic writing and communications skills needed to develop blogs that both attract and satisfy the information needs of your readers.

- Finally, as a successful physician or aesthetics business owner, you are self-motivated.

In this case, you have the passion and drive to do all of this work yourself. When you do – assuming you have that passion and drive – you'll be surprised at how easy it is to accomplish all of the steps involved.

The second approach – the collaborative approach – is often adopted by already over-stretched doctors and aesthetics business owners. In this case, instead of doing the work yourself, you collaborate with a professional writing coach, a co-writer or ghost-writer who will help to get your book or eBook written.

This professional communicator will help you take your ideas and experience, then translate that into the blogs, white papers and case studies that will become the basis for the book or eBook.

These professional communicators will also help you with creating Social Networking's audio-visual parallels – video blogs, YouTube videos and webinars), all focused on ultimately converting that same information into the chapters, sections and sub-sections of your published book or eBook.

You can work with a co-writer or ghost-writer; however, if you're an effective and self-motivated writer, you can certainly take these steps and execute them yourself. If you do, you'll create your own published book or eBook in far less time than you expect it to take.

Having decided to proceed with creating a published book or eBook by using the Social Networking Foundation Approach, here are the steps you'll take.

Your book begins with a concept, a theme, a central idea. This is the message which you passionately want to share with your patients or clients. That concept becomes the spine of the entire social networking/book/eBook process.

An example of "theme" can be found in a ghost-written book we produced for and with a gifted breast cancer researcher – "*New Hope for Breast Cancer*."

This book was written to help this academic surgeon move from a New York Medical University into a Palm Beach private Medical Practice that focused not only on treating breast cancer, but also on post-treatment aesthetic breast restoration. Its nine chapters included an introduction and a conclusion – as well as seven chapters on seven pending or just-over-the-horizon breakthroughs.

Written for the patient and her family, this book was produced in a readable "layman's" style, but with all the authority of this gifted professor and researcher.

So the first thing we do is to come up with a focused topic that will help to meet your Medical Practice-building goals, along with a dynamic and attention-getting title. This should be catchy – but it should also define the information you want to share. The title should also help to define the market and audience you want to reach.

Once we have nailed down a useful and informative focused topic, along with an eye-catching title, we next create a very detailed table of contents. Experience has shown that for a straightforward topic, a minimum of seven to nine chapters is often sufficient to present the material. However, that length is remarkably flexible.

Regardless of the ultimate length of the eBook, the first chapter will be a summary – it will tell the readers what you're going to cover in the book. Then the middle chapters will actually present the real in-depth content. Finally, wrap it all up in a tight and informative summary that comprises the final chapter.

A note for budding authors who would like to create a series of follow-on books, know that – if you plan the book properly at the outset – each of the chapters can be expanded into its own book or eBook.

Think of how John Gray turned "*Men are from Mars, Women are from Venus*" into a dozen or so books, each describing how this one basic relationship concept can be made to work in the board room, in the marriage bed, when dating again and in many other interpersonal arenas.

Just as John Gray did with his series of books (and just as the Chicken Soup guys did the same thing by creating more than 175 spin-off books), you can expand your initial book's chapters into a series of useful in-depth published books or eBooks on more narrow topics.

But that's down-the-road, for the future. Let's continue to look at how we can create your first book.

First, as noted, the subject and the title. Then an in-depth, detailed outline of what will be covered in each of the chapters. Then, before you start writing, break down each of the chapters into a more detailed outline that covers the content in each chapter's sections and sub-sections.

That's actually a pretty standard approach used by many writers for creating almost any kind of non-fiction book.

However, we're talking about creating a published book or eBook using the Social Networking Foundation Approach, and that means we'll be using a host of social media tools to present the book's information far and wide over the Internet, long before the book itself is completed.

That's at the heart of our Social Networking Foundation Approach – publishing the information several times in several different formats, then stitching together what we've already written together into the final book.

This approach will result in building your reputation among future book readers *even as you write your book.*

As we create the book's content, blog by blog, white paper by white paper, we'll be laying the groundwork for your publishing success, which will occur once the book or eBook is completed and ready to either sell or give away.

This leads us to one of the true secrets of our Social Networking Foundation Approach.

Basically, as we develop your book's content – writing and posting the blogs, case studies, the white papers and other material that will ultimately be used as the building blocks of the book's chapters, sections and sub-sections – we keep writing and presenting that same very useful (to the readers) material, not once, but over and over again.

The content material first presented in a series of blogs becomes the basis of the case studies and white papers, as well as their video equivalents. Then, all of these published social networking content become the core material for the book's various chapters and sections and sub-sections.

In short, we use social networking content like building blocks, and build each content level on the previous ones, in the process creating a "Social Networking Foundation" of content.

For instance, five blogs become a white paper or case study, then three white papers and case studies become one of the book's chapters.

Using this Social Networking Foundation Approach, there is a remarkable economy of creative thought and effort here. The basic ideas we work together to develop will be presented several times, in several different formats.

As noted, each of these formats will appeal to a certain kind of content consumer. Some prefer the relatively casual approach of blogs, others like the nuts-and-bolts of case studies, while still others prefer to see their content information visually – as a video – rather than having to read it in print format. Yet in each instance, the core information remains the same.

Here's how we do it

After having created the concept, title and detailed outline for the book, we proceed as follows. For each section or sub-section of your book, we first interview you – our client/author – for anywhere between 45 minutes and two hours at a sitting. In these interviews, we obtain the background information we need in order to write the blogs, white papers and case studies that then become sections of the book.

Each interview becomes a collaborative brainstorming session. As professional interviewers, we "challenge" our authors to think beyond the basics of the outline, perhaps unearthing ideas or information not anticipated in the outline.

This is always valuable, and usually winds up enhancing the depth and value of the building blocks that lead to the Book.

To make sure we didn't misunderstand this information, we then write up the interview and share it with you to confirm that we understood the information presented. Once you clear our notes, we take that interview material and write it down in a series of several different content formats – blogs, white papers and case studies, which we publish and promote in a variety of Social Media.

We also work with you to create the video equivalents of that content. Finally, we then convert that material into book chapters.

That's the "secret sauce" of the Social Networking Foundation Approach to writing a published book or eBook. We repurpose the basic information in a variety of formats, publishing and promoting it online by making use of the most popular Social Media platforms.

Doing this, we build an audience – and receive valuable input from the target audience – before converting it into a book that already has an eagerly-waiting audience.

By the time we get around to writing the Book, we have a thorough grasp of the content, and have "experimented" with presenting it in several formats. In our experience, this has always enriched the final material, helping to ensure that the book is as good as the subject matter and the writer's communications skills can make it.

To move the development of the material leading to the book forward, we tend to schedule these interviews at a regular time, generally once every week or two – but certainly at least once a month. Even the busiest professionals or business owners – if they're serious about creating a published book or eBook – will adjust their schedule to permit these interviews.

Some interviews are conducted over lunch, that being a time when even the busiest individuals generally take a break. While doing this during business hours has obvious advantages, some interviews are scheduled in the evenings or on weekends.

Recognizing that it's more important to maintain a regular schedule than it is to find a convenient time during the business day, we flex our schedule – sometimes doing interviews at night or on weekends.

For most of our clients, we do the writing for them, serving as their co- or ghost-writer. We do this, first, because we're experienced writers. However, we also do this so our clients – especially if they're not comfortable serving as writers – don't get bogged down in the process of writing.

Our clients are busy medical professionals or aesthetics business owners, and while they are motivated to create a published book or eBook – or even a series of related published books or eBooks – they find that day-to-day priorities of their professional Medical Practices or businesses tend to push the book into the "priority backwater."

That's a value we add to the process – we keep it moving forward on a schedule that ensures the book gets written and published.

When we work with our clients, generally their roles involve reviewing and editing what we write – the blogs, white papers, case studies and their video equivalents – as well, ultimately, the book. Obviously, our clients have to take a more "visible" role (pun intended) in producing their video blogs, YouTube white-board videos and webinars. Still, they rely on us to create the scripts, the talking points and outlines for their audio-visual presentations, and to oversee the production as well.

To enhance our clients' blogging "reach" – and to help them attract new readers – we also search out other blogs, by other writers, covering the same material to be included their books.

We then add respectful comments to these "competitive" blogs. In these comments, we either agree with the blogger, then add a new point or two – or, we very respectfully disagree, then explain that disagreement briefly and concisely. In this way, we can "borrow" other bloggers' audiences without violating the unofficial – but very real – code of ethics that dictates successful Social Networking.

There are three keys to this process:

- Be respectful to the blogger we comment on

- Add value with our comments

- Include a link back to our own blog-site or website

Whether we agree or disagree, this is an effective and legitimate way of leveraging other blog-writers' followers. We'll be persuading them to check us out – not by any sales pitch, but by virtue of the quality of our comments. These comments demonstrate that our clients are also worth following.

Cutting to the chase, this is legitimized poaching, one of the few ways of co-opting others' followers that is both accepted and approved of by the Social Networking community.

Re-Purposing Content

Having conducted the interviews, we first write up the material in blogs and their video offshoots.

Then we convert that material – generally from several blogs – into white papers and case studies, as well as their video offshoots.

Let us emphasize that: in the Social Networking Foundation Approach, these white papers and case studies cover the same basic material as is found in the blogs.

However, that information is presented in different formats to meet the information needs of a largely different set of readers. The same information is given to them from a different perspective and in a different writing style.

But at the bottom line, it's still the same material, presented in different formats, and therefore attracting the widest audience.

Take a moment to absorb this. It's critical to this whole Social Networking Foundation Approach to writing and disseminating published books or eBooks. We keep re-using the same material, presenting it in different formats, the better to suit the information needs of different people.

Each time we rework the same core information, you gain additional followers and further enhance your reputation in your own market niche.

Formats: As a rule of thumb, blogs – along with video blogs and comments on other writers' blogs – tend to be conversational and relatively informal. However, white papers tend to be a bit more formal, and, with links to sources and even a list of "further reading," they can have an almost academic tone and feel.

Case studies tend to be practical and pragmatic, with nuts-and-bolts information, as well as – frequently – either direct or indirect testimonials.

As noted, this same approach translates well into the audio-visual format. White board presentations can effectively cover the material found in white papers, while webinars tend to be effective in presenting case study and testimonial information.

These video formats are flexible and will vary from topic to topic, as well as from author to author. The key is to translate the information from blogs, white papers and case studies into video presentations that work for your audiences.

Promoting Content
PR and Social Networking Conversation

Having used and re-used the information in varied formats, let's now look promoting this content.

Each time we publish a blog or post a video blog (or submit a blog comment) for one of our clients, and each time we post a white paper or case study for downloading from your website, we then promote this new content. We do this first online, via conversational posts on Facebook and LinkedIn, as well as through Twitter tweets (making use of hashtags when appropriate) – or, if you're material is visual, Pinterest.

We also use professional PR techniques to build audiences and awareness for this content, but let's focus first on Social Networking promotion.

Social Networking Promotion: To promote each new piece of content, we use these various more conversationally-oriented social media sites. We've found that you can get by with something no more complicated than a "check out our new blog" posts on these social networks, though we also provide more in-depth and "motivating" posts as well.

Right from the start, in advance of creating these posts – especially for LinkedIn and Facebook – we first have our clients join discussion groups that cover the topics related to their forthcoming books. We don't just join on behalf of our clients – we create posts that contribute to these online Social Media groups.

This is a critical part of the "Conversation" element of Social Networking, and will give you credibility – as well as some advanced visibility for your book – when we then post an invitation to check out your new content.

This pre-established credibility is critical to building a following in the social networking world.

And it works.

We find that, for each new published piece of content, when we post several different promotions/invitations on Facebook and LinkedIn, we generate followers.

To further the process, we then create as many as seven different Tweets promoting each new piece of client content, each tweet targeting a different element of the content, and each tweet also focusing on a different segment of the likely audience.

What this amounts to is a steady and reliable volume of conversational communications – what advertisers call 'reach and frequency' – that, taken together, help generate audience interest for your Social Networking content, and ultimately, for your book.

For a single piece of content information, we have already created:

- Three to five narrowly focused blogs – each of which also has a companion video blog – which leads to ...

- One white paper, along with a YouTube video, perhaps a white-board presentation – which leads to ...

- One case study and a related webinar, and, finally ...

- A chapter or sub-chapter in your book

Then, we'll also create and post on your behalf, for each piece of content:

- Three to five different Facebook invitation posts, shared among a number of groups; and,

- Three to five different LinkedIn invitation posts; again shared among a number of groups; and finally

- Five to seven different Tweets promoting the content for different reasons and to different audiences.

If you're into numbers, this approach means that each chapter of the book will be based on up to 14 distinct content posts, each of which will then be promoted online 13 different times.

This creates a total of 182 "conversation" promotion posts for each chapter, even before the book is written.

Do the math – before we ever write a single chapter of your book, the "word" on that particular chapter will be out in the Social Networking universe – the "blogosphere" – 196 discrete times.

That's a lot of pre-promotion for your book.

PR Promotion: However, we have learned that, to significantly further enhance the impact of any really meaningful or "seminal" content you create, we also use conventional media public relations to further get the word out. Using wire-service press releases, for instance, we'll be reaching audiences you're sure to miss with your online promotions.

We'll also be reaching the news media which covers your market, building awareness among them that you're an expert with a book in the works.

This PR process begins when we write and issue a press release on your behalf, promoting one of the new pieces of content. We typically send these out via BusinessWire, which is – for what we intend to accomplish in boosting your online following and media awareness – still the best release distribution service in the business.

BusinessWire puts your information out in an entirely new venue – Google-searchable news.

One not-well-known reason for using BusinessWire – it has contracts with roughly 300 news aggregator sites, including Yahoo Finance and MSN. This means that every press release is guaranteed to be posted at least that many name-recognizable news websites.

That also does your SEO efforts a lot of good, but the primary purpose is to attract new first-time readers who'd otherwise never have heard of you, and to put you out there where interested media will become aware of you.

While many bloggers use social networking to promote a new content posting – and we'll do that for you, too – relatively few bloggers ever consider using PR.

Properly executed, professional media-oriented Public Relations has a huge potential for attracting new followers who would otherwise never find your content. This is achieved by creating and issuing provocative press releases to support each of those new content posts.

In every promotion post on any social network, and especially in every press release – we will be sure to mention that this material is from your forthcoming book, "*Title*."

That will get your book's name out, and add credibility to whatever content you have created, published and promoted.

In addition, the media is always looking for new and fresh "experts" who can put the news into context for their audiences.

Taking advantage of that media need, whenever your topics touch on breaking news topics, we will use our media contact lists to pitch local and national talk radio and talk television producers and hosts, offering you as a published expert in the topic. Here's an example of how this works:

> In 2008, testing this as a new concept, on behalf of a client who was interested in politics as well as medicine, we first developed five specific controversial and informative business-related topics that were tied to that year's Presidential election.

> Next, on behalf of that client, we wrote up each of these topics as articles or blogs and secured their publication in a prestigious online news-and-commentary "e-zines." We then contacted the producers at several media outlets and pitched our expert on the topic of the day – including a link to our published write-up on that topic.

> Five for five, we secured for our client interviews on Neil Cavuto's program on Fox Business, as well as five interviews with Imus.

> Our client also appeared on 56 other radio talk programs across the country. Finally, one article was read in its entirety by Rush Limbaugh on his high-rated national talk radio program, one that had 20 million listeners per week.

> In short, by leveraging an online blog or article covering an intriguing and newsworthy topic, we were able to create for our client appearances on a significant number of national and regional radio and television programs.

This same approach can work for almost any author.

For example, through effective public relations, we were able to take something we wrote for our client on a breaking-news topic. Based on that write-up, we landed them interviews on CNN and MSNBC, and a guest editorial in USA Today.

This then generated write-ups in the editorial page of the New York Times and more than 75 other daily newspapers.

What made this significant is that, just the week before, the client had published a new book, with a press run of 5,000. Within a week after these media appearances, the client had sold out the entire press run of the book, which then went into a second printing.

Since this was a self-published book, this phenomenal sales level generated more than $125,000 in profits for our client, the executive director of an Atlanta-based healthcare-related not-for-profit.

There are no guarantees, but this kind of PR process is certainly worth the effort – especially when you have something newsworthy and – perhaps – a bit controversial to say. Success is easier to come by especially when the media perceives you as published author.

The bottom line – we use all these various avenues available to you to legitimately promote each new content posting. Each promotion will ultimately help you, in large ways or small, to promote your book or eBook, as well as to help build your Medical Practice or business.

The Social Networking Foundation Revealed

This whole Social Networking Foundation Approach is really very simple and logical. However, when we first developed this concept, we were frankly amazed to find how often these steps are overlooked by other bloggers, and even by successful authors.

Once again, here is how it works: after each interview, we use the information generated, not once, but over and over again.

In the process, we create a content Social Networking Foundation that focuses on building an audience while creating an impact – in essence, making the maximum use of each chapter and sub-section in the forthcoming published book or eBook.

The chart below may help you visualize how it works:

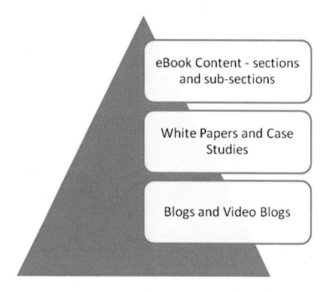

Two key elements of the Social Networking Foundation Approach that this graphic doesn't show are the way we re-use content (up to 14 times for any given book or eBook chapter), as well as the ways we promote each new published piece of content (up to 196 times online, along with aggressive and effective media-oriented PR activity).

That creates a great deal of useful online activity, all focused directly or indirectly on your forthcoming book or eBook. However, because we'll keep re-working and re-packaging the same basic material in different formats for different audiences, we'll accomplish a great deal of useful and ultimately profitable activity with only a relatively little bit of actual "new" creative work.

Taken together, the Social Networking Foundation Approach ensures that you have both the "content" that is one half of the Social Networking experience, along with the "conversation" part of the equation.

When combined, and when based on truly useful and informative content, we will position you as an online guru, a true "subject matter expert" who will attract respect, recognition and new patients or clients.

This new approach to leveraging both "content" and "conversation" to build an audience in the Social Networking field – all designed to turn you into a Subject Matter Expert and "Thought Leader" – will help you focus on your own eBook success. If you have all the information you need to create the content and handle the conversation, go for it.

However, if you'd like help in turning yourself into a published author – and a powerhouse in your specialty area – then find an experienced and prolific writer who is ready to help you, as coach and interviewer, or as co-writer or ghost-writer.

When you're ready, as Star Trek's Captain Picard said, we're ready to work with you to "make it so."

beautiful forever
Aesthetic Business Consulting

Appendix

Attached are a number of tools useful to Medical Practice-builders.

beautiful forever
Aesthetic Business Consulting

Appendix One: Event Checklist

Before you schedule an event – before you start planning an event – review this checklist to make sure you've got everything ready that you need, including all of the decisions that need to be made. Then keep this checklist handy and review it often to make sure you're still on-target for a successful event.

Defining Your Event

- Decide on the purpose of your event; make sure that every part of the event – from pre-event promotion to at-the-event hand-outs to after-the-event follow-up – reflects that purpose.

- Identify one key person in your office who will take ownership of your event – not to do it all, but to make sure that it all gets done, and done right and on-time.

- Identify Your Venue – factors to evaluate:

    o   On-site or off-site?

    o   How large an event are you planning?

        - Note: Larger events requiring off-site facilities will often require a 3-4 month lead time on a venue.

- Develop a detailed invitation for your event.

    o   Email and Print Invitations

- The invitation should include the date, time and place, along with a motivating and intriguing topic.

- The invitation should be created to reflect your "brand identity."

- Create a VIP list of patients, a local referral list, and media list

- The invitation should include follow-up contact information – RSVPs aren't required.

- Develop a mail-to guest list. Test the list for "bounces" or returned mail.

Large Event Guest Contact Timetable

- Sixty days prior: send a "Save the Date" pre-invitation to potential guests. If budget permits, send both an emailed notice and a surface-mail postcard notice.

- Forty-five days prior: Mail formal invitations to your guest lists. Also send out an email reminder the day you drop the invitation in the mail, "look for our invitation to our event."

- Two weeks later (i.e. 30 days before the event), for those who haven't already returned an RSVP, re-send the detailed invitation again, this time with a personalized note. Once again, send out an email reminder the day you drop the invitation in the mail, "look for our invitation to our event."

- Two weeks pre-event, if you still have unanswered invitations, call the guests and extend a personal invitation. The day before you start the calls, send them a "head's up" email.

Small Events Guest Timetable

- Three to four weeks prior: Post a notice of the event in office and on social media – and begin taking reservations.

- Two weeks prior: Distribute invitations via email blast.

- One week prior: Repeat the email blast.

Soliciting Vendor Support

- Favorably leverage your relationships with your own vendors – get them to underwrite as much of the cost as possible.

- Network your event among your vendors.

- Create a version of your invitation to be displayed at your strategically-allied businesses.

- Forty-five to sixty days pre-event: Send your vendors an email inviting their participation and support.

- Ask specifically for door prizes and other add-value support from your vendors.

Getting The Word Out

- Use your social media sites to announce the event and invite/encourage participation. Example: Facebook Event Page

- Encourage responses through your website. Your website should have an event link.

- If seats are limited then attendance at this event should be by invitation or pre-registration only – encourage RSVPs.

- Create an incentive for guests to "bring a friend." Example: Door prizes valued at $2,000.

- To effectively promote each event, and beginning thirty days in advance of your event, take advantage of free marketing:

  o Send out a press release to your entire media contact list
  (If you need assistance with your press release contact *beautiful forever*)

  o Send out a notice to your chamber of commerce list.

- Plan on door prizes; gift certificates, gift baskets or a specific highlighted treatment are examples of good door prizes.

- Swag Bag. Everyone leaves with a gift bag and practice goodies.

- Most of your guests will anticipate refreshments; so, while considering your budget – and your event theme – plan on appropriate refreshments.

Getting Your Office and Staff Ready:
Two Weeks Till Event Time!

- Hold a Staff Education Meeting to review and focus on procedures you may want to promote at your event.

- If you are holding your event in your office, on the day of the event, schedule patients in the morning – but not the afternoon or not at all. Office staff must be prepared and ready.

- Off-site Events: Two weeks before the event, confirm facility, product vendors, caterer, rentals, etc. All arrangements should be complete and confirmed 10-14 days prior to event day.

- Create a to-do list that covers both the week before and the day of the event – and include day-after follow-up:

  o Thank you notes for attendee.

o   Confirmation of booked appointments.

o   Perhaps an extension of the "night-of" discounts for people who wanted to "sleep on it" before deciding to have a procedure.

- Designate a person/s in charge of check in and registration, and make sure they completely understand their role, including gleaning contact information from walk-in guests.

- Menu of Services and Event Night Special Prices to hand out.

Day of Event

- Review with staff the event flow, event goals, and special offers. Make sure they understand their role at the event.

- Upon check-out, all attendees should receive a "swag bag".

- Offer 'this **night only discounts**' for attendees who book at the event. It will help them decide – that night – to come in later for specific treatments.

- Have Menu of Services and Event Night Specials sheet available to promote and sell at event.

   However, as noted above, be prepared to extend the offer in your follow-up email, for those who need to "sleep on it". Example: 25% off procedures night of event. Extend 15% discount if booked within four weeks of event.

- In Office Event: have soft, mood music playing. Decorate with fresh flowers. Obviously, the office should be spotlessly clean. All displays should be in place and organized.

- Off Site Event: Plan to arrive at venue at least 4 hours prior to event to setup displays, confirm that everything is ready, handle last-minute glitches (there are always last-minute glitches – plan on them and don't let them fluster you).

- Have your staff dressed appropriately for the event, and consider the theme of the event when determining what is "appropriate."

- Display relevant brochures, as well as before-and-after pictures – your own (preferably) or stock photos provided by allied vendors.

- Patient flow should be directed by a concierge or greeter (with name tag).

  - Office tour of your facility

You can use your practice manager for this, or even bring in a professional, such as someone from the cosmetics department at an upscale department store.

  - Have models and rooms setup with demos to perk interest and promote more guests

- The area where staff members are taking money for products, gift-certificates, etc., should have a price list available for all the procedures – with special prices being offered that night and discounts on gift certificates both prominently displayed on the price sheet.

- To handle visitor flow, depending on the amount of people attending (40-60 makes sense), you will need two people taking money and giving clients instructions and two people making appointments.

- Doctor and key staff should be available to speak with guests, providing explanation of services, answering questions, etc.

- Optional educational power point or presentation 10-20 minutes. Leave time for questions and answers. Photos of before and after sell all procedures.

After The Event

- Be sure to include your list of attendees as part of your e-mail blasts and direct mail campaigns

- Send "thank you" messages to attendees

- Follow up with people who had sent in an RSVP, but who didn't show and offer a free consultation.

Now all you have to do is do it again. And again. And again.

beautiful forever
Aesthetic Business Consulting

Appendix Two: Event Planning
Define Your Event

Preliminary planning for your event will assist in determining your event goals, timeframe and budget. Complete the questionnaire below

Defining Your Event

- Purpose (Goals and Objectives) of Event:

- Event Financial Goals:

- Event New-Patient Goals:

- Brief Description:

- Target Date or Dates:

- Number of Attendees Desired:

- Venue Rental Required? (yes or no)

- Event Coordinator and Contact Info:

- Participating Vendors:

- Event Budget:

- Have you or a staff member planned an event of this type? (yes or no)

- Have you considered a staff appreciation bonus for a thank you? (yes or no)

- Have you contacted an Event Planner? (yes or no)

    Contact **beautiful forever** team if you need coaching for your event.

Sample Event Calendar

MONTH	THEME	DESCRIPTION	GOAL
January	New Year/New You Girls Night Out	Homecare discounts; Packages and Series type offerings; BOTOX and Filler discounts.	Advertise broadly to attract NEW patients and mine your patient database to capture clients who have not visited you in the past 3 to 4 months
February	Love the Skin You Are In Mens Night Out	Play on Valentine's Day. Utilize patient database and website to advertise event and promote new procedures.	Utilize patient database and website to advertise event.
March	Seminar: Non-Invasive Skin Rejuvenation Time to promote Laser Resurfacing	Create a presentation that ties together your complete offering for Skin Rejuvenation: Homecare, injectables, laser treatments, aesthetician treatments. Offer packages that combine these offerings	Education: Educate current and new patients on your practice treatments and protocols for young looking/healthy skin. Offer discounts to book packages at the time of the event.
April	Summer Ramp Up Beach Party	Focus on treatments for the body: Hair removal; Waxing; Body Wraps, etc	New Patients: Hand distribute event flier to businesses with complimentary services/products. Invite their VIP's and offer special discounts
May	Mother's Day Event	Remember Mom's by offering buy one get one 1/2 off skincare treatments for all who schedule to come in with their mothers	Mind current patient base - email blast. Offer Gift Certificates and Package Specials
June	Introduce a new procedure	Repackage current offerings or introduce a new product/service	Education: Patients and Potential patients LOVE something new. Educate them on your new treatment and offer discounts to book at the time of the event.

July	TAKE THIS MONTH OFF: Evaluate Events to date; Regroup and make sure you have followed up!		
August	Back to School/Teacher Appreciation	Catch educators before they go back to work and Moms who will now have a bit of spare time	Advertise broadly to attract NEW patients and mind your patient database to capture clients who have not visited you in the past 3 to 4 months
September	Sponsorship of Local Charity Event	Reach out to the community by sponsoring a charity event. Have a presence at the event!	Name recognition of your practice in the community
October	Partner with a local business to put on a joint seminar	Target patient lists from both businesses to double the reach of attendees.	Current and New Patients - introduce your patients to a local business who offers a complimentary service or products.
November	Head to Toe for the Holidays OR Christmas in November	Holiday "spruce up" packages including BOTOX and fillers, skin brightening microderm and peels, décolletage treatments, manicure/pedicure combos	Advertise broadly to attract NEW patients and mine your patient database to capture clients who have not visited you in the past 3 to 4 months. To sell more gifts/gift certificates.
December	Patient Appreciation	Kick off the holidays with an early in the month event to thank your core patient base. Invite only!	Invite Only! Top clients are invited to attend and bring a friend for special discounts and raffles.

beautiful forever
Aesthetic Business Consulting

Appendix Three: Mystery Shopping Checklist

Website

- What core message does the website project?

- Does the website answer your questions?

- Is the website easy to navigate? Could you easily find the information you wanted?

- Does the website "invite you" to call for an appointment?

- Overall impression

Call for appointment

- Was the call answered within three rings?

- Did the phone receptionist sound like she was glad to hear from you?

- Did she seem knowledgeable?

- Did she answer your questions professionally?

- Did she make you want to make an appointment?

- Overall impressions

Location

- What kind of impression does the office location present?

- What does the lobby tell you about the Medical Practice?

- Was the lobby crowded or comfortable? Quiet or noisy? A good place to fill out forms, or lacking in privacy?

- What does the Medical Practice signage say to you about the Medical Practice?

- Overall impressions

Reception Staff

- Were you greeted right away, or did you have to wait?

- Did the receptionist act like she was glad to see you? Or did you feel that you were an interruption in her busy day?

- Did the receptionist seem knowledgeable?

- Did the receptionist answer each of your questions professionally?

- Did the receptionist make you glad you made an appointment?

- Overall impressions

Registration Forms

- Did the forms include the practice's graphic logos and the practice's name? Were these forms professionally designed?

- Did the questions the forms asked make sense? Were you asked to repeatedly answer the same information questions more than once?

- Did any questions make you uncomfortable? For instance, were you asked if you'd ever sued a doctor?

- Did these forms ask why you'd come – specifically, what you wanted?

- Did these forms ask how you'd heard about the doctor or the Medical Practice?

- Overall impressions

Information Hand-outs

- Were you provided with hand-outs with useful take-home information?

- Did this information look professional?

- Were the hand-outs made for the Medical Practice, or did it seem generic?

- Were the hand-outs "branded" for this doctor's Medical Practice with the practice's name and graphic logo?

- Overall impressions?

The Office Consult

- Did the doctor create rapport?

- Did the doctor seem to care about you and your specific needs?

- Did you feel welcome, or did you feel like you were an intrusion on the doctor's busy schedule?

- Did you feel rushed, or did the doctor take all the time you needed to have your questions answered?

- Did the doctor seem to listen and to respond to your comments, questions and concerns, or did the doctor have a standard approach?

- Did the doctor review your needs and desires within the context of the doctor's services?

- Did the doctor ask why you wanted these procedures and what outcomes you hoped for?

- Were the solutions the doctor offered responsive to your needs? Or did those solutions seem to be "one-size-fits-all?"

- Did the doctor explain the procedures you might be having, including the risks you'll be taking, as well as the expected results?

- Did the doctor make you feel confident about his or her skill and ability?

- Overall observations or impressions

The Sales "Close"

- Did the doctor handle setting up the treatment procedure appointments and other arrangements, or did a staff member handle the review of the procedures, the cost and the terms?

- Did the doctor or staff member seem focused on your needs, or on selling you a package?

- Did the doctor or staff member ask about your timetable?

- Did the doctor or staff member ask about your financial situation?

- Did the doctor or staff member try to "close you" on the spot (i.e., sign you up for a procedure on the spot) or did he or she just provide you with information?

- Overall impressions

Consult "Follow-Ups"

- Did you receive a follow-up call, email or letter from the doctor or a staff member?

- Was this follow-up professional?

- Did this follow-up make you want to schedule a procedure? Did it seem "commercial" or did it seem "caring?"

- Overall impressions

Overall impressions

- Did the visit to the doctor improve your perception of the doctor?

- What was your overall impression of the doctor?

- If you were going to have a procedure, would you use this doctor?

- Would you refer this doctor to others?

- Overall impressions – sum up your experience.

beautiful forever
Aesthetic Business Consulting

Appendix Four: Secret Shopper Call Questions

Date:
Time of call:
Name of Person (answering telephone):
Office:
Beautiful Forever Consultant:

Did the person who answered the phone call identify the Medical Practice and her name?

☐ No   Poor
☐ Partly   Average
☐ Yes   Good
☐ Yes, with enthusiasm!   Excellent

Did the person answering the phone ask for your name or any contact information?

☐ No   Poor
☐ Only Half   Average
☐ Yes all of it, but when almost done with the call   Good
☐ Yes, at the beginning of the call   Excellent

Did the person who answered the telephone ask where you heard about them?

☐ No   Poor
☐ Kind of   Average
☐ Yes   Good
☐ Yes, and asked specifics (which TV show, magazine, etc.) Excellent

Did the person who answered the phone address the following question: Why would I use this particular doctor? I have 2 other doctors that were recommended to me.

☐ No/Ignored   Poor
☐ Answered but did not provide much info   Average
☐ Answered explaining basic reason   Good
☐ Yes, very supportive of Medical Practice and gave very
    specific reasons why I should come to this Dr vs. another   Excellent

Did the person who answered the telephone ask you your areas of concern (what areas you are looking to get treated)?

☐ No   Poor
☐ Made assumptions   Average
☐ Yes & asked more specifics   Good
☐ Yes & affirmed it was a popular (great) treatment area   Excellent

Did the person who answered the telephone ask you if you knew about how the procedure works?

☐ No   Poor
☐ Asked but did not provide much info   Average
☐ Yes & asked more specifics, explaining basics   Good
☐ Yes & explained basics, common tx areas, and affirmed   Excellent

Did the person who answered the telephone ask you to come in for a consultation?

☐ No   Poor
☐ Yes, but asked a closed ended question
    (yes or no answer)   Average
☐ Yes & gave suggestions for open days/times for consult   Good
☐ Yes & asked best time of day for you, following up two
    options for dates & times that are within 72 hours   Excellent

Consultant comments:

beautiful forever
Aesthetic Business Consulting

Appendix Five: *beautiful forever* Services 2015

beautiful forever List of Services - 2015
☐ General Consulting – Information & Questions
☐ Project Management
☐ Full Day Practice Assessment/or Evaluation on site by a senior consultant that will determine project direction and implementation, including a comprehensive report with findings and recommendations
☐ Brand Discovery Session: a two-day in-depth assessment of a company and/or practice that is conducted by the senior executive marketing team. This process uncovers the key differentiating points and business objectives to produce a strategic marketing, PR and branding plan
☐ ½ Day Practice Assessment
☐ General on-site visits to review staff, revenue reports, etc.
☐ Business Plan- (Bank ready): 　○ Competitive Analysis 　○ Feasibility Study 　○ Demographic Analysis 　○ Financial Projections 　○ Industry Overview 　○ Business Description 　○ Market Analysis 　○ Strategic Marketing Plan Overview 　○ Financial Analysis and Forecast
☐ Pro-Formas, including P&L, projected start up costs and cash flow projections- 5 years

☐ Creation and Management of Project Timeline
☐ Funding Assistance
☐ 12 month or 18 month strategic marketing plan/budgets
☐ 12 Month Implementation of marketing, branding and PR
☐ Assist Operations Review- Expenses, Inventory
☐ Productivity Analysis
☐ Business Development Concepts- Create Blue Print to roll out your program
☐ Marketing & Communications Support   o Strategic to Tactical Marketing Planning, including budget & timeline

☐ Practice Events-Plan- Determine Goals
   o Create Theme
   o Market/Promote w/Custom Invite, Evite, Eblast, Flyers, Posters, Specials
   o Tracking
   o Follow up

☐ Public & Media Relations, including Press Releases and Media Events
☐ Assistance with soft and grand opening preparations
☐ Customized Promotional Products

☐ Custom Printing and Mailing Service
   o Invites-Design/Print/Stuff/Mail within 24 hours
   o Flyers/Postcards-Design/Print/Mail within 24 hours
   o Brochures-Design/Print
   o RX Pads-Design/Print

☐ Custom Printing and Digital for the Web
   o Magazines with 2 Page Feature Article/Design/Print/Mail
   o Before and After Books (Hard and soft covers)/Design/Print

☐ Social Networking, including:
   o Blog Writing
   o White Papers & Case Studies
   o Scripting Video Blogs

☐ Assistance with Staffing- screen, interview, and recruit employees

☐	**Training - operations, sales, service, and management**
	  o **Front Desk Training and Scripts**
	  o **Coaching Practice Coordinator**

☐	**Employee Manual and Contracts**
☐	**SOP Manual Customized**
☐	**Job Descriptions, compensation plan**
☐	**Mystery Calls with Report Card (series of 3)**
☐	**Mystery Shop Onsite Program**
☐	**Identify and assist with selection of computers, and software**
☐	**Coordination of purchasing of equipment and supplies**
☐	**Assist Architect/Designer with floor plans & design element**
☐	**Concept Design & Floor Plan Review**
☐	**Compliance for surgical centers & existing spas that want to have operating rooms**
☐	**Legal and insurance assistance**
☐	**Website evaluation (free call to review findings)**
☐	**Assist with web-site design**
☐	**Develop, Create, Customize Script for On-Hold message**
☐	**On-Site hands on operations turnarounds**
☐	**Consulting Time sold in packages of 5 hours- to consult or advise on business development or to help answer questions**

In addition to these services, *beautiful forever* offers:

beautiful forever **University:** This online university offers ongoing professional development education programs. Operated in conjunction with some of the top businesses in the industry – all eager to help physician Medical Practices and medical spas succeed – we offer a range of hands-on learning courses designed to be put into practice.

The programs offered by BFU are valuable to all private medical practices, not just those in the aesthetics field.

Go to the ***beautiful forever*** website (www.beautifulforever.com) and link over to the university for more information, and to register for the best practical education in our field today.

Aesthetic Medical Success System: An updated version of my ground-breaking book on aesthetics marketing and business practices, which has been sold through the ASPS for the past four years, is now available from ***beautiful forever***.

This is a complete educational guide to building, managing and marketing of a cosmetic Medical Practice or medical spa.

This 500-page system complete includes:

- Concept Creation

- Business Plan Template

- Selecting a Market Niche

- Architectural Designs and Floor Plan

- Creating a Menu

- Equipment Selection

- Branding

- Marketing Manual

- Legal and Insurance issues

- Operating Efficiently

- And Much More

- A CD of 12 customizable forms

beautiful forever
Aesthetic Business Consulting

Appendix Six : Press Release Example

PRESS RELEASE
FOR IMMEDIATE RELEASE
PR CONTACT: (name)
PR PHONE: (number)
LAJOLLA, CA- March 22, 2006- (WHO) Dr. Michaels of The Michaels Aesthetic Practice (WHAT) has become fully accredited to perform the procedure name, the first aesthetic technology to improve smile lines. Interested consumers can attend Dr. Michaels' seminar about procedure name (WHERE) at the Michaels' practice on (WHEN) April 10, 2006 at 2:00pm (WHY) so that they can make better educated decisions about procedures that can improve smile lines, one of the most popular areas of elective-fee-for-service medicine today.

The First and Following Paragraphs

After the first paragraph, it is important to develop the story in greater depth. Use the inverted pyramid structure, proceeding from the very basic information to the very detailed. This style helps the editor who can then cuts information from the bottom of your press release, if necessary, without sacrificing essential content. At the bottom of your content, center ### to let the reader know the release is at the end. Following this ensign, include an About The Doctor Biography.

• Keep it simple, use short active words, sentences and paragraphs. Denote the reasons why the listener should consider the procedure, doctor, etc. (before and after photos and patient quotes are critical). You'll also want to recap of the main message at closing, repeating accreditation information, phone number and website address information.